Patterns and Coincidences

Patterns and Coincidences

A Sequel to *All Is But a Beginning*

John G. Neihardt

University of Missouri Press
Columbia & London, 1978

Distributed by the
University of Nebraska Press
ISBN 0-8032-3312-4

University of Missouri, Columbia, Missouri 65201
Library of Congress Catalog Card Number 77-24199
Printed and bound in the United States of America

Library of Congress Cataloging in Publication Data

Neihardt, John Gneisenau, 1881–1973.
    Patterns and Coincidences.

    1. Neihardt, John Gneisenau, 1881–1973—Biography.
2. Poets, American—20th century—Biography.
I. Title.
PS3527.E35Z523 1978   811'.5'2   77–24199
ISBN 0–8262–0233–0

The lines from "Lonesome in Town" are reprinted from *Lyric and
Dramatic Poems* by John G. Neihardt by permission of University
of Nebraska Press; copyright 1913 by *Poetry: A Magazine of Verse;*
copyright 1915 by *Forum;* copyright 1915, 1916, 1919, 1921, 1926
by Macmillan Company; renewal copyright 1954 by John G.
Neihardt. The lines from *The Song of the Indian Wars* are reprinted
from *The Twilight of the Sioux* by John G. Neihardt by permission
of the University of Nebraska Press; copyright 1925 by Macmil-
lan Company; copyright 1943, 1946, 1953 by John G. Neihardt.
Article concerning marriage of John and Mona Neihardt is re-
printed by courtesy of the *Omaha World Herald.*

These—Gaki's last—writings are dedicated
to his most recent great-grandchildren:
Janette Marie, Allison Leigh, Heather May,
Christopher Marquis, and John
to whom, and to all "playmates" everywhere,
his message was:
I shall be young with you.

Publisher's Foreword

Patterns and Coincidences is the second and concluding volume of John G. Neihardt's autobiography. It picks up exactly where the first volume, *All Is But a Beginning: Youth Remembered, 1881–1901,* ends—at the sacrificial burning of *The Divine Enchantment,* the first of his published book in 1901. It ends in 1908, when his career as a mature writer and his life with his family was beginning to develop.

Neihardt was a poet; among the honors accorded him was the title of Poet Laureate of Nebraska. But in being a poet, he was also an observer of the culture of the Indian and white man in the American West during the nineteenth and twentieth centuries. His most famous work, the prose narrative *Black Elk Speaks,* the story of the Sioux up to their crushing defeat at the Battle of Wounded Knee through the eyes of a very old and very holy Oglala Sioux, is certainly a testament to his keen observation. And all of his poetry is his story of the rapport he held with the West and Midwest he grew up in and lived in throughout his life.

All Is But a Beginning and *Patterns and Coincidences* are that same story, but through the eyes of Neihardt as chronicler looking at his own experience rather than from the more objective perspective of poet or biographer. In it he shares his rare "moments of insight and wonder" because, as he humbly relates, "It is not assumed that the life story of an ordinary man is of sufficient interest to justify the telling." It is not a chronological account of his entire career but lingers in reflections on the past and goes beyond the chronological ending of the story with glimpses into later significant developments in his life.

This volume of the autobiography was completed shortly before the author's death in November 1973, at the age of ninety-two. Hilda Neihardt Petri, one of his daughters, is responsible for pursuing the publication of Neihardt's last chronicle of the land he lived in.

Contents

1.

Introduction to Mature Years

Those who may be acquainted with the "youth" section of this testament, ending with the ritualistic burning of my first printed book, *The Divine Enchantment,* have noted that I am not presenting a chronological chain of events faithfully linked in one-two order. Rather I am concerned with rare moments that may be called high spots of experience—moments of insight and wonder, moments of comedy, of happiness or sorrow, of pain, of beauty, or even of beauty in pain—as I shall have occasion to remember when the time and mood are right.

Thus it is not assumed that the life story of an ordinary man is necessarily of sufficient interest to justify the telling. But surely in the high spots of any life the human spirit may rise momentarily to meanings worth the sharing.

My youth and the grand old nineteenth century ended together with the sacrificial fire. As I look back now it seems that I became a different person at that time, with a revolutionized world view. I have long thought and previously remarked in a wondering, exploratory manner that somehow there are dynamic spiritual patterns in our cosmos, that destiny is a matter of being caught up in such a pattern, apparently by accident, and of being compelled to strive for its realization in the stubborn stuff of this world, be it for good or ill.

Somewhere in the mysterious region of highly improbable things there is a very remarkable little book entitled *Patterns and Coincidences*. It has never been written, but I have read it in cursory fashion and with sufficient understanding to know that it explains many baffling occurrences now called chance. But there it is, waiting in the sifting dust of time for some creative soul to come along and translate it into the idiom of our crude world.

When I was still quite young and understood a great many things, I promised myself that I would write this neglected little book of light. I could still write it, old as I am, and until a short while ago I still hoped to honor my youthful promise; but it has been getting later and later recently, and now, with apologies to my youth, I must default.

2.

The Passing of the Gods

I had experienced a sort of cleansing glory in giving my precious little book to the flames. But the glory soon faded in the commonsense light of day and left me desolate in a world gone empty. There were times when I actually considered deserting poetry for some more practical worldly interest, but the thought only left me sick at heart. Then one white night when I lay awake pondering questions without answers, the heavens opened for me again. The dynamic pattern for a major poem that I had abandoned came back upon me with a new surge of power. It had haunted me day and night for some time before the Virgin Devanaguay and her Divine Son had taken me over completely. Now it returned with much of the old excitement to fill my world again.

The Passing of the Gods. Surely it was a magnificent conception. Obviously both the title and the idea were suggested by the Scandinavian *Ragnarok,* the destruction of the Norse gods, or its Germanic equivalent, the *Götterdämmerung.* But in my plan the idea was given general scope and significance not limited by geographic or seasonal considerations. I would include all the foremost deities of the world pantheon. Even now, after these many forgetful years, I can see it all vividly as when I was a youngster. Sometimes I have even indulged in a vain, momentary desire to give it being yet.

I can see it now—the flowing host of gods that lonely man, lost in the cosmic mystery, created in his need. Of wonderment and terror he created them; of loneliness and loss; of longing and despair—the long parade of obsolete and obsolescent gods that man had made and worshiped and outgrown. Emerging from the dreadful dark they came, a luridly self-luminous procession, tunneling the night of time. Slowly they passed before me, one by one, under the brilliant glow of now, to fade away and vanish in the dusk of ages. And then—the Man of Sorrows, still bent beneath the burden of his cross, still bound for new Golgothas.

Before I fell asleep that night I had decided to write *The Passing of the Gods,* using the Spenserian stanza as my medium. Good Spenserians are almost as difficult as Petrarchan sonnets, and I could have saved myself much effort by choosing blank verse. But I was fascinated by the gemlike quality of the strict stanza form when well fashioned. Also I had noted, as the result of much practice, that the very difficulties of structure, when fairly mastered, greatly increased the economy and power of expression.

The next day I began work on the poem; and for several years thereafter it furnished me with my principal excuse for being alive.

I had given up teaching as a possible career and was living with my mother and sister, Lulu. We had moved from Wayne to Bancroft to make a home for Lulu, who was teaching in the local school. Jobs were scarce and paid little. I did anything I could get to do for a little money. Occasionally the *Bancroft Blade* could use me on its job press or in bringing the weekly paper out on time. But sometimes I was idle when I could not write a line and the glory left me. At such times I nursed the sickening fear that maybe, after all, I was only a misfit and ne'er-do-well, living off my mother and pretending to be a poet. I must have presented some such image of myself to some of my fellow townsmen in those days. "The Poet's Town," written years later when the memories of that time were no longer painful, was more or less reminiscent of that period of my life. By that time, however, I was able to generalize my experiences, giving them impersonal and enduring significance.

3.

The Hod Carrying

During the spring and summer of 1901 I was able to prove myself well beyond self-doubt or possible public scorn. The local brickmason and plasterer hired me to carry the hod for him, although I was scarcely heavy enough for the grueling job. I weighed only 120 pounds; and a hod full of mixed mortar could have weighed little less, if any. The mason and I were well acquainted and, of course, he knew about my athletic stunts. The wages agreed upon were hardly a determining factor in hiring me, for I am sure he could have had much heavier men for the fifteen cents an hour he paid me.

That was a record-breaking summer as I have reason to recall, the temperature reaching an all-time high of 104° in the shade. We often dozed out the midday swelter, working late in the cooling off of the evening. Baker plaster was sold in hundred-pound paper sacks; and I sometimes carried ten sacks of plaster, mixed with two parts and and water, in a twelve-hour day.

Silly as it now seems, my boss and I were actually working in competition—he, the master "mechanic" as he liked to think of himself; and I, the mere groundling who had a lot of serious proving to do. If I managed to heap more "mud" than usual on his mortarboard, he went immediately into violent action, smearing plaster on lath like a champion. Once when we were finishing the upstairs rooms of a German farmer's new house in the country, my boss, aloft yonder, began shouting, "Mor—*tar! Mor*—tar!" with an insulting upward twist on each syllable in turn, seeming to imply that I had been loafing long enough in the pleasant shade; and now how about a little honest work for my wages?

I had been doing my level best, and a little better, to maintain a steady flow of plaster; and as the English professors would say, I had been "busting a gut" on that nefarious stairway. Members of the medical profession have told me that I am what they would describe as the "adrenal man," and when I heard that insulting demand for even greater effort, my suprarenal glands must have gone into action. I could feel the hair standing up on the back of my neck, and I was no longer weary.

The man said mortar, did he? Well, he should have it.

He had been working on steaming hot ceilings all that forenoon, and I knew that he must be nearly "all in," but being reluctant to admit as much, he was passing the burden of delay on to me.

"Mor—tar! Mor—*tar!"*

"Coming up!" I shouted.

Falling furiously to work, and sustained by that gadfly voice from above, I mixed a generous batch of plaster. Then I began delivering at a brisk gait.

The first hodfuls were received in mock surly silence, but when the heaped plaster began rolling over the edges of his mortarboard and the hods kept coming, he began protesting in earnest. What in the unholy name of "Helen Highwater" did I think I was doing! Couldn't I see he didn't need any more plaster just then? By the—et cetera.

So I yelled "M—o—r—tar" and set out at a dogtrot

for another hodful. This time I staggered drunkenly on my way up those stairs and I was barely able to stumble up to the mortarboard and dump my load.

Somewhere in this faithful history I have found occasion to mention the now-lost art of picturesque imprecation, otherwise described as fanciful and innocent cussing; and I believe I named my boss as a champion practitioner of the art, then flourishing.

The excess mortar around the box was ankle deep and greasy. One of us must have slipped, for all of us—my boss, the full hod, and I—went down together in a muddy mess. Finally scrambling to our feet, our arms locked about each other for support, we rocked with the silly, helpless laughter of exhaustion. It was when he regained his breath that he delivered one of his characteristic diatribes. I cannot remember the whole oration and would not repeat it if I could, but the beginning ran something like this: "By the blue-jointed, jumping Jehosaphat and the bald-headed Moses—."

One morning shortly thereafter my boss did not arrive early as usual. I mixed a batch and sat down to wait, wondering what could have happened. Still he did not appear. I made a neat pile of mud on his mortarboard, placing his apron, hawk, and trowel nearby, that he might go to work at once upon his arrival, making the most of the lingering morning cool.

I was about to go in search of him, thinking he might be sick, when he turned up, looking as though he had just finished a hard day's work in the heat.

"We won't work today," he said, his face quirking as with tears unshed. "We lost the baby last night, John. I'll spread this batch, and then I wish you would go home with me. I'll need you to 'tend me tonight, John, setting up with the baby and all. Maybe the woman can quit crying and get a little rest if you come."

My career as a hod carrier ended in early August when, thanks to the eloquent recommendation of Willard Sinclair, owner and editor of the *Bancroft Blade,* I was offered a job as reporter on the *Omaha Daily News.* I had occasionally contributed short articles to the *Blade,* and, as a result, Sinclair was convinced that I would one day be "heard from," and it was a great pity that I should "blush unseen and waste my fragrance."

I sincerely regretted leaving my boss, for we had become like pals since the long night together with the baby. But the call of destiny seemed unmistakable. Even the offer of five-cents-an-hour wage increase could not hold me. When a heavier man was available at the offered price, I accepted the Omaha job with enthusiasm.

4.

City-Hall Reporter

Joseph Polcar, city editor of the *Omaha Daily News*, struck me as the most handsome man I had ever seen. Tall, perfectly proportioned, he carried his weight with the easy grace of an immortal, as I liked to think (or perhaps a champion boxer?). And such was the Olympian dignity of his mien that I was shocked to hear a common mortal of the staff address him airily as "Joe."

My briefing was brief indeed and pointed. After I had found my way about, I would be tried out on the city-hall run. Reporters were expected to contribute to the Sunday paper in addition to their regular duties—feature articles, human-interest stories, unusual items of news. Sunday copy must be turned in no later than Friday noon. First, "Jim" would show me about town for a day or two to help me find my bearings. My salary would be nine dollars a week. Then my new boss wished me good luck and dismissed me with a widely inclusive wave of the arm, as though to say, "Well, there's your world and it's your oyster. See what you can do with it!"

Jim was more explicit. When we set out on our urban odyssey, he said to me, "Now my boy, first of all, I will have you know that if you want to be a good news hound, your two best friends will be a soubrette and a hack driver. They know what is going on, and they will talk to a friend." During the next two days I learned something of what he meant as we circulated in and out of strange places, meeting equally strange people. Everywhere Jim was hail-fellow-well-met. Apparently he was somewhat in the nature of an institution, with no family name to separate him from the multitudinous Smiths and Joneses of the world. Nor did he seem to need one, being so definitely and unmistakably "Jim."

That afternoon we arranged for what was to be my future home. The "For Rent" want ad offered "a light housekeeping apartment" on the third floor of the old Calumet Cafe building. As a matter of fact, it was a crudely furnished attic room, complete with sink and running water, with a skylight as the sole source of illumination. Jim thought it would be a good place to write poetry, for which, I surmised, he had only a token respect. Also the *Daily News* was only two blocks away; and the price, three dollars a week, "with linens furnished," was most inviting to one of my foreseeable income.

Another three dollars would furnish my board, since a filling meal of baked beans and fried liver with onions could be had for a dime—no extra charge for bread or a second cup of coffee. Occasionally a man might visit one of the more affluent and generous bars, there to purchase with an ordinary nickel a steaming cold goblet of Oh-Be-Joyful, the size of a gas globe. Having sipped awhile in a nonchalant manner, one might indulge in a free lunch of cold cuts and roast beef and pickles, together with tempting and thirst-provoking tidbits. If one boldly ordered a second draw, he might even have a notably courteous colored gentleman to slice and serve the roast. However, woe to the lingering glutton, who might find himself more or less graciously escorted to the side door. But for a scarcity of nickels and dimes, those were the halcyon days indeed. At such prices a man with reasonable frugality might accumulate a tidy sum against possible future necessities.

As I think of it now, that attic room was a den of horrors, full of slinking, ever-changing shadows until the nooning day began to seep through the dingy ceiling glass. Then only were the oil lamps entirely superfluous. But I was having a romantic adventure in the big city, which could just as well have been Paris, except for accident—Victor Hugo was my current literary god, and I was still under the spell of *Les Misérables*. It was easy to fancy Jean Valjean living incognito up there among the chimney pots. (There really weren't any, but the expression somehow thrilled me.) And it required little effort to visualize poor, pretty little Cosette panting wearily up those steep, long flights of stairs.

Although Jim had faithfully introduced me around about the sacred precincts of city hall, I was never made to feel that I really "belonged" there. I was pretty much the lost cat in a strange alley. Somehow it seemed there was a dark secret abroad that eluded me. Items of municipal news that had seemed important to me failed to make the columns of the paper, and I lacked the brass to ask why. Often I was ingloriously "scooped" by an article on some event in my territory that was certainly news to me when it appeared in the paper.

But, although city hall remained a mystery, I was fairly able to hold my own in the Sunday edition. An anonymous weekly column that I had intended to be funny did attract a few readers, I was told. Also I contributed some articles about "queer" people whom the writer was supposed to have met in his rambles. These, however, were entirely, even impudently, synthetic.

I recall the highly improbable but allegedly well-authenticated saga of the professional "hospital bum" who specialized in acute public attacks of a mysterious malady that had landed him in half the emergency wards of the country and stumped many a distinguished physician. This ingenious rogue had developed his specialty, it was said by those who should have known, into a veritable fine art. He could produce with blood-curdling fidelity the whole ghastly process of dying, right up to the penultimate gasp of agony. It was even told on competent authority that he could control his heartbeat for realistic effect. This, however, had been seriously questioned; but it was offered, nevertheless, for what it might be worth to interested parties. There were some moderate repercussions in the letter column, I believe.

Soon after the above news item appeared, President McKinley was assassinated and my "hospital bum" was immediately forgotten in the national mourning for "our martyred president." The poem I wrote on the subject promptly appeared as one of many minor items in a column of the daily edition. I do not recall the slightest indication that anybody ever read it. But I did have the satisfaction of seeing it hiding in the midst of the loud world's recorded agitations.

Nonetheless, I had been making progress in my one-room apartment. Often when I should have been penetrating the dark mysteries of city hall, I was busy adding finely carved Spenserian stanzas to my *Passing of the Gods;* and I was genuinely happy doing this, for I still regarded the poem as probably the chief justification of my short (?) life. Surely there were times when my one-room attic apartment (complete with sun and moon and stars by skylight) was next-door neighbor to heaven!

But it was getting to be later than I knew, as we shall see.

Every weekday morning each reporter found beside his typewriter a bunch of news clippings borrowed from other papers. These were to be rewritten in disguised form, and if need be amplified, for our evening edition. I must confess that I was rather handy at that relatively innocent form of petty larceny. Among the clippings there was often a special assignment.

On the morning now recalled I found among my purloined items of news a brief account of an accident that resulted in the death of two children and their father. Attached to the clipping was a note that read: "Follow through—interview if possible. Copy no later than noon. J. P." A brief address followed.

Having arrived at the address in what must have been record time, I found myself unable to ring the doorbell there below the black bow of mourning. Twice I stole up to the curtained front door and twice I turned away, fleeing on tiptoe from the heartbreaking sound of a woman crying within.

When at length I came before J. P. to give my report, he looked me over curiously in silence for a while, then said: "Well?"

"I couldn't do it," I replied rather lamely. "There was a woman crying inside and I just couldn't do it."

That evening I was scooped again.

It was not until several days later that the ax finally fell. I was sitting at my desk in the newsroom, halfheartedly trying to pound out something for Sunday, when the voice of J. P. came booming through the clatter of gossiping typewriters.

"Neihardt!"

A heavy silence spread over the room, and all faces turned toward me.

I went to him at once and stood waiting while he looked me over. "Neihardt," he continued at length, "I guess we will not need your services after today. You haven't made good at city hall. Your Sunday stuff is all right, but we need a city-hall man just now. Sorry."

"Yes sir," I replied. It seemed the only thing I could say.

I felt green sick and I wanted out of there forthwith. As I turned about and started for my hat and coat, the chattering of the typewriters began again with what seemed to me a new self-conscious emphasis. I was aware that all faces were turned again to the machines with exaggerated fixity of attention.

And so, seeing my services were no longer required, I took my leave. But that is only part of the story.

My abrupt retirement from a journalistic career occurred in the fall of 1901. Twenty years later I was on a nationwide lecture tour, reciting my poetry at colleges and universities.

I had gone far since my McKinley poem. My *Bundle of Myrrh,* a sequence of passionate love lyrics, had attracted much attention, as far away as Paris, where it found my Mona and made her my wife. *The Stranger at the Gate,* a lyric sequence celebrating the arrival of our first child, and *Man Song,* a miscellaneous collection of verse, had given me considerable reputation. When the first narrative poems of my *Cycle of the West* appeared, my readings were in demand across the country.

In the spring of 1921 I had been made Poet Laureate of the State of Nebraska by legislative enactment, and this too had occasioned much publicity. It was the first time any poet had been so designated by a legislative body.

My next engagement was in Omaha, Nebraska, where my *Song of Hugh Glass* and *Song of Three Friends* were being studied in the high school that was sponsoring my appearance there.

Evidently the youngsters were making much of the event. When my train pulled into the Union Station, hark and behold! The high-school band, in full dress for the occasion, turned loose with an earsplitting version of *The Stars and Stripes Forever.*

Oompha-boom, oompha, boom, boom, boom!

When the impassioned rendition ended with a clash of cymbals and a definitive bang from the big bass drum, the principal of the high school made a short speech of welcome. He then introduced His Honor, the Mayor, who proceeded to say extravagant and glorious things about the hometown boy who made good.

Then a tall, handsome man with a shock of gray hair and a broad smile stepped lightly forth from the welcoming group. His remarks were as concise as his briefing of me had been just twenty years before:

It was his pleasure to announce that I had been appointed editor in chief of the Daily News *for a day—the date to be chosen by me. During my editorship I would be the conscience of the paper, selecting the news and presenting it to the public in keeping with a poet's sense of values. The staff would give me all needed assistance. I would be paid at the rate of nine dollars per week until a more suitable compensation could be arranged.*

I thanked my old boss, expressing genuine regret that I must reject the offer, owing to previous commitments.

How I wish I could have accepted, with the distinct understanding that I be given a thoroughly competent city-hall man—preferably himself!

And what fun it could have been to manipulate the news! I can almost see the front page with its brazen eight-column bannerline all about some self-sacrificing deed of one hitherto obscure John Jones (or maybe Annie Smith, the scrubwoman). Just to scan either story would make one proud of the human race. As for accounts of crime and meanness, they would be found in the back pages, faithfully set forth in eyestraining agate type.

And I can almost hear the newsboys shouting: *"Pay-peh! Pay-peh! Four-star edition! Read all about the bravest and kindest act in history! Latest news of the Jones family (or the Smiths). Pay-peh, Mistuh? Only two cents. Tanks, Mistuh! All about—."*

But I see that my tale has outrun the telling here on this farseeing height of time. Although I could not know it then, my destined victorious return to the scene of my disgrace was still twenty years deep in the future yonder. It was only waiting to happen when the stars were right, after much toil and trouble. So there was nothing for it but to take my hat and leave with some small balance of my pay.

There were no stars in my skylight that night. It rained. A slow, chill, sighing rain. I lay awake for a long while, wondering what to do next. I longed desperately to go home but the thought shamed me. I knew that my fine job in the city had occasioned much comment, kindly and otherwise, around our town. And what would be said if I came slinking home like a beaten dog with dragging tail? There were moments that night when even hod carrying seemed a delightful occupation.

Lulled into a pleasant drowse by the monotonous drone of falling water overhead, I began idly making rhymes as a soporific. It was better than counting sheep. The groping after fitting words and their happy mating in singing sound and meaning made me forget to be homesick.

> The dull day wanes, the fog shuts down,
> The eaves trough spouts and sputters;
> The rain sighs through the huddled town
> And mumbles in the gutters.

Huddled town! The line shocked me wide awake. It seemed so pat an example of the fortunate epithet. *Huddled!* That was how the town looked with its deserted streets, its windows and doors tightly closed against the chill and damp.

So I went on expanding the picture.

> The emptied thoroughfares become
> Long streams of eerie light;
> They issue from the mist and, dumb,
> Flow onward out of sight.

> A crowded streetcar grumbles past,
> Its snapping trolley glows;
> Again where yon pale light is cast
> The hackman's horses doze.

> In vain the bargain windows wink,
> The passersby are few;

The grim walls stretch away and shrink
In dull electric blue.

A stranger hurries down the street,
Hat dripping, face aglow;
O happy feet, O homing feet,
I know where mine would go!

The last thing I remember that night was imagin-
ing myself out on my uncle's farm when the cows
were coming in.

For there, far over hills and dells
The cows come up the lane,
With steaming flanks and fog-dulled bells
That tinkle in the rain.

Or should it be *muffled?*—no—*fog-dulled* was better.
That tinkle in the rain—or could they really *tinkle* in the
foggy rain? Or did they actually *tonkle?* Or maybe
tinkle-tonkle?—no—that would need a little more
work.

Then suddenly wan morning was seeping down
upon me through the skylight. The rain had ceased.

Before going out on the prowl for breakfast I sat
down, wearing my topcoat against the lingering
chill, and began writing down the lines I had fash-
ioned, more or less tentatively, during the night. In-
cidentally, I discarded the onomatopeic experiment
tonkle, fearing that Webster was not likely to be co-
operative in the matter.

Then, with all my vocal stops pulled out, stressing
consonants and singing vowels, I gave the poem
aloud to the applauding hollow of my attic.

It was with a light heart that I went forth into the
hopeful, rainwashed day. Why should I feel dis-

couraged? Surely I would find some way to make my modest expenses if I only tried hard enough. No doubt the editors of *The Youth's Companion* would want my latest and probably my best poem. Already they had published my "Song of the Hoe," written in a potato patch, and even paid real money for it, at fifty cents a line. And had they not asked to see more of my work? Any day now I might receive their acceptance of my "Song of the Turbine Wheel" submitted about a month ago? It was a far better job than "The Hoe" verses, which I had come to regard as utterly without beauty and perhaps a trifle silly.

And then what about my prose story entitled "The Tiger's Lust," that I had intended to offer as a contribution to the Sunday edition of the *Daily News?* Although unfinished, it was all dreamed out to the last detail. I even knew the last sentence. Maybe I could sell it to the *Philadelphia Ledger.* The *Ledger* was a weekly paper largely devoted to sensational fiction, and it had an enormous circulation for that time. On Saturdays ambitious small boys, taking the traditional first rung of the presidential ladder, hawked it noisily up and down the streets of the nation at a nickle a copy.

As I was passing the front of the Calumet Café on my way to a ten-cent eating place, I saw a sign in the window, "Porter Wanted." Although it aroused unpleasant memories of another sign in another restaurant window, it did ring a bell in my head.

While finishing my fried liver with a free second cup of coffee I made tentative plans for a triumphant future and an honorable return to Bancroft.

There was no difficulty in making a deal with the café proprietor. I would begin work at 5 P.M. acting as a busboy until the restaurant closed at midnight.

6.

Adventure with Death

My description of the Beecher's Island fight in *The Song of the Indian Wars* contains a passage that I sometimes repeat to myself for the feeling of release and exaltation it still gives me as when it was written many years ago.

Forsythe's fifty scouts are holed up in the sand of a small, low island in the Rickaree, nervously awaiting the command to open fire on a band of eight hundred Cheyenne charging in a solid formation astride the shallow stream.

>   "Wait!" the Colonel cried;
> "Keep cool now!"—Would he never say the word?
> They heard the falling horses shriek; they heard
> The smack of smitten flesh, the whispering rush
> Of arrows, bullets whipping through the brush
> And flicked sand *phutting;* saw the rolling eyes
> Of war-mad ponies, crooked battle cries
> Lost in the uproar, faces in a blast
> Of color, color, and the whirlwind last
> Of all dear things forever.
>   *"Now!"*
>   The fear,
> The fleet, sick dream of friendly things and dear
> Dissolved in thunder; and between two breaths
> Men sensed the sudden splendor that is Death's,
> The wild clairvoyant wonder.

When I wrote those lines I was not drawing altogether upon imagination but attempting to describe certain experiences of my own. I came into this world a bit too late to take part in any of my Indian fights. But I have come close to the other world on several occasions, and each time I felt the same sense of release and exaltation.

The first time it happened to me was shortly after the arrival of the robins. The spring wheatlands had turned a vivid green, and meadowlarks rejoiced in the pastures. I was in my early twenties, and death was the last thing I'd be likely to think about. My boss had sent me into the country selling hail insurance, and it was good to be out of the office after a long winter. The pair of Hambletonians I drove were as happy as I, prancing and fighting the bits, for they had done little else recently but chomp their feed and nip each other. Accordingly they were ready to run at the slightest provocation. For instance, when I playfully touched the spokes of a spinning front wheel with the whipstock just to see what they would do, they did it! Both inferred at once that we were in a Roman chariot race *and losing.* It took considerable *whoa-ing* and bit sawing to restore a respectable carriage gait.

And what a spanking team they were, as we used to say in the good old pre-motor age when we and the world were young. I like to recall how beautiful they were when they responded to the driver's cluck and flick of the whip, setting up the musical phasic rhythm of hoofbeats for a thrilling dozen miles per hour—if the roads happened to be good.

And to see their blond manes stream in the wind of their going!

Well, we came to a prosperous-looking farm home with a windmill whirling merrily in the backyard. The front gate being wide open, we turned in for a good cold drink after the run. There was a plowman in a nearby field, and he might well be good for a nice policy on his promising wheat crop and on the corn he would soon be planting yonder. I headed the team into the angle between the barn-lot fence and the well enclosure. Then I wound the lines loosely about the standing whipstock and stepped down out of the buggy, thinking to unhook the checkreins of the horses that they might drink at the overflowing trough. They seemed safe enough for the moment, headed into the fence corner with the running water to hold their interest.

I was perhaps ten feet from the buggy seat when a smart-aleck colt in the barn lot came squealing and bucking explosively up to the fence corner to greet and tease the new neighbors. Apparently the colt's rude remarks and rowdy behavior were regarded as insulting. The team reared, screaming, and swinging sharply away from me took off at a loose trot for the open gate. I was close behind but not quite close enough; and the speed of the team was increasing. If I could only reach that whipstock, now on the far side of the buggy, before they went into the gallop!

My chance came when they were forced to slow down momentarily for the short turn into the open road. I took a diving leap for it and was aware that the buggy toppled, bouncing crazily in the square, wheel-cramping turn. Somehow it kept on its wheels and I knew with a sick clutch of terror that I was lying on my right side, my neck across the left front axle, my face close to the whirling spokes. I was gripping the handhold on the buggy seat above me with one hand and loosely holding the lines with the other. The left foot was in the buggy bed, the other hanging.

We were in the open road now and "going for the doctor" at a gallop soon to break into a run if I didn't get them stopped. The lines were useless in my head-long position by the wheel. I was trapped, apparently with no way out. This, I thought, was it! I was going to be killed, and it would all be over soon. Nor did it seem to matter.

Then an overwhelming sense of expanded being and clairvoyant awareness swept through me. I could see my predicament and its many implications with vividly luminous clarity and complete acceptance; and somehow it was good.

I know what happened then, but I don't know how. There was a diagonal streak of dust across my chest that must have been made by the tire of the left front wheel when I went over. I had turned over in the air and landed facing forward, my heels firmly planted in the dirt road, the lines tightly grasped in both hands, my body slanted backwards against the plunging of the horses.

When at last the team stood still, panting, I was barely able to crawl into the buggy; but I felt glorified by what I had just been through. For a measureless moment *I had accepted death as an exalting experience.*

On two other occasions I have known that sudden enlargement of being when it seemed I was about to leave this world forever—once in the fast water of the Missouri River above Fort Benton, Montana; and again at the dizzy edge of a cliff in the Kaibab Forest in Arizona.

In feeling about for words to describe the experience, I am reminded of what an old Sioux told me about his first sun dance. As he leaned against the torturing thong in his chest, dancing and praying, he said, the whole world went black, and he was lost in endless night. But he kept on dancing and praying; and all at once there was light everywhere, and he could see everything.

"And what *did* you see?" I asked.

"Everything," he said with a look of awe in his face—"Everything!"

Remembering my experience, I think I can feel what he meant but could not tell—and neither could I.

I know that such states may be caused by the injection of adrenaline into the bloodstream under great emotional stress. But is it not possible that such a state, so induced at the near approach to death, may reveal reality transcending our commonsense world?

I have come to think so.

7.

With Caryl and the Longhairs

It has been apparent that my first acquaintance with the Omaha gave me a conception of that mythical abstraction, "the American Indian," very different from "the noble red man" of the romantic sentimentalist. Reservation Indians, as I first saw them with no historical perspective and out of cultural context, seemed as little noble as they were red. It was two or three years before I came to know and respect the Omaha as an ancient people with a rich culture that was dying out with the old, unreconstructed longhairs, to be remembered only as a matter of curious interest.

I had become well acquainted with the Farley brothers, Caryl and Jack, who were grandsons of Iron Eye, the last head chief of the tribe, and nephews of the La Flesche sisters, Susette (the famous Bright Eyes) and Susan (Dr. Picotte). Caryl and I were often together on business at the agency, and we became good friends. He had a sly sense of humor expressed less by his sparing utterance than by the twinkle of his piercing black eyes, and I never think of him as laughing. When we had nothing better to do, we sometimes engaged in a wrestling bout. He was a short, stocky man of about my height and age, and he had been put together like a bull calf. I can't remember our ever wrestling to a fall, for the very good reason that I was always busy evading his attacks.

It was thanks to Caryl that I began to be on friendly terms with the old-timers of the tribe. One evening he took me with him to a private feast and dance given by old Shonga Ska (White Horse) for some of his friends. The affair was held in a wooden lodge, built after the fashion of the ancient earth lodges, with the same turtleneck entrance, the circular room, and the fireplace at the center under the open smoke vent in the roof.

A babble of voices ceased abruptly as we entered. Cross legged in a ring about the fire, over which a hanging kettle steamed, sat a dozen or so old men and women. On the far side of the circle sat our host, with wrinkled face and thin white hair. Evidently he had expected us, for after hailing us as friends, he beckoned us to places in the ring. Then two old men brought us tin cups full of beef soup from the steaming kettle.

When we had eaten together, Shonga Ska began humming an air as though to himself, beating a light accompaniment on a drum held in his lap. The humming grew into singing words that loudened with the drumbeat, and one by one the guests joined in till all were singing. It was a song of welcome, Caryl said, and we must stand and thank them, which we did. The language didn't matter in the least, for the men all cried *how, how,* and the women made the tremolo with their palms upon their mouths.

Much of the evening was spent in visiting, but now and then someone would start another song. The drumming would begin, and pairs of women, each with an arm across the back of the other, would dance side by side about the ring with a modest, shuffling step. Once a toothless patriarch, evidently indulging a wry sense of humor, tottered to his feet and clumsily aped a few steps of an athletic war dance that brought forth happy laughter and left him muttering and panting in his seat. "He is explaining," Caryl whispered in my ear, "that he can't dance very well anymore."

Once old Shonga Ska held up a hand for silence, and when all were still, he pointed to me and said, with Caryl interpreting: "This is a good young white man who has come to visit with us. He respects us. He sits and eats with us as a friend, and he makes us glad. He is a good young man." That was an accolade indeed, for Shonga Ska was highly regarded by his people.

Shortly thereafter a grandmother of notably ample dimensions got up from her seat, waddled about the ring to where I sat and, grasping me by the coat sleeves, lifted me bodily to my feet. Then, having pulled one of my arms across her back as far as it would reach, she began to teach me the woman's sliding, shuffling step. The drum began again with increased enthusiasm, and there was good-humored laughter as we danced together; for I am a small man, and it was clear that Grandma had never watched her waistline.

8.

Dr. Susan Picotte

As a result of my growing acquaintance with the older people, I wrote a number of short stories on Omaha Indian themes. These were highly imaginative experiments in the use of the Indian idiom, both in conception and expression. Perhaps because they differed so greatly from the conventional "Indian story," the old *Overland Monthly* of San Francisco bought several of them.

It was these stories that brought me the friendship of Dr. Susan La Flesche Picotte. Dr. Picotte was the first Indian woman to receive the M.D. degree. She was the oldest of the four La Flesche sisters, including the once-famous Bright Eyes. They were the daughters of Chief Iron Eye (Esta-maza, Joseph La Flesche).

When I first met Dr. Picotte, she was practicing medicine, mostly among her people, with an office in her Bancroft home. When she happened upon my stories, she wrote me a note, asking that I come and see her. I went with my heart in my mouth, for from my viewpoint at the time she seemed a most austere personage. Tall, slender, black eyed, as I remember her, she bore herself with an air of dignified authority that made her seem far less gentle than she proved to be.

I had often seen her on the street and knew her as Caryl's aunt. I had heard her speak in public—an experience to be remembered. She spoke simply, and she had a most effective way of increasing the impact of a climactic sentence by withholding it in silence overlong. During such a time, one could feel the tension building in the audience. Her face grew lighter, and she seemed to vibrate with intensity of feeling. Then, in a low voice, she said it!

I had become fairly well known among the Omaha as Tae-Nuga-Zhinga (Little Bull Buffalo), and she greeted me by that name, noting my friendship with her nephew. Then she spoke of my stories, and forthwith my heart went singing back to its proper place in my breast. She liked them! She even said that mine were the only Indians in literature from Cooper to Remington that had not been offensive to her, adding that she could not understand how a white man could represent the Indian idiom so perfectly in the English language.

I have had my share of praise in the more than sixty years since then, but none of it has meant more to me than those words of Dr. Picotte. The product of two widely different cultures, she had lived, as a child, the primitive tribal life of the Plains Indians, and as a woman, she had been socially received by the Brahmans of Boston.

I was quite well acquainted with the doctor's husband, Henry Picotte, a mixed-blood Sioux, whose father was related, I believe, to the aristocratic St. Louis Picottes. It was easy to see how the Omaha Indian girl, Susan, could fall in love with Henry, for he was a handsome man with polite, ingratiating manners and a happy sense of humor. In his later years, when I knew him, it could be said—and was —that sobriety was not always his principal virtue. But, sober or otherwise, Henry was good company, and he could tell a story with the best of them. I recall especially his mimetic account of a youthful escapade in a circus sideshow.

According to the barker, he was a veritable wild man only recently captured in a Borneo jungle at great peril to the captors. Stripped to the breechclout and chained to a stake in the ground by way of protecting the customers, it was his business to wolf chunks of bloody meat and growl ferociously. One day this had been going on for some time when a corpulent lady of obvious importance marched boldly up to him, pinched his naked arm, and said: "Young man, you can't fool me. You ain't no wilder than I am. How long you been civilized?"

"I scratched my head awhile and thought hard about it," said Henry. "Then I said, 'Oh, 'bout three weeks, ma'am'!"

"They fired me without pay, for that one!" said Henry.

9.

The Bright Eyes Story

The most famous of the La Flesche sisters was Inshta Theamba (Bright Eyes), the wife of Thomas H. Tibbles. I knew her three sisters and her brother Frank, but I never met Bright Eyes in life, although we lived for some time in the same community; and it is probable that she was only casually aware of my existence. But my memory of her is one of the most vivid and strongest among my cherished recollections—and also one of the most beautiful. It happened thus:

Tibbles was editor of the Populist weekly, *The Lincoln Independent,* and for some years he and his Indian wife had lived in Lincoln, Nebraska. But, owing to her ill health, they had recently moved to Bancroft, making their home on her Omaha reservation allotment four or five miles north of town.

When I arrived on the scene, the name *Tibbles* was being bandied about here and there—on the street corner, in the barbershop, in the homes no doubt. And it was plain that, in the sober judgment of solid citizens (like ourselves), the man wasn't quite respectable. For he was brazenly opposed to instituted authority and the time-honored rightness thereof. A self-proclaimed Populist, he was really no better than an anarchist, some declared. Why, he even advocated the free coinage of silver, much to the consternation of responsible "moneyed" men.

But I was in my reckless early twenties and far from certain that the cockeyed, suffering old world didn't need a bit of strenuous fixing. I had seen hungry men begging for jobs and glad to work a ten-hour day for a dollar. I myself had worked in the beet fields for less. I had seen corn used for fuel in the bitter-cold winter, because the bottom had dropped out of the market at eight cents a bushel, and no buyers. I had seen my hardworking farmer uncle raising food enough to board a regiment and growing poorer and poorer, unable to keep pace with the galloping interest payments. Also, in the disparaging gossip there were recurring overtones that made the man a romantic figure for me.

I remember a bull session in the drugstore when Tibbles was being dismembered by a committee of the whole, and I remember remarking, with little credit to myself, I'm sure, that when almost everybody seemed to "have it in" for a man, I felt I must get acquainted with him. At the least calculation, he must have something special to distinguish him from the rabble—if only an improved technique for horse stealing.

So I did manage to meet him; and we readily became friends, for he was a lonely man.

In the evening after the news of Bright Eyes's death had spread abroad, a farmer from north of town, whom I knew only slightly, drove up to my home with a written message from Tibbles, his neighbor. He would be sitting up that night with his dead wife, and he would be most grateful if I would come and keep him company. Of course I went, naturally supposing that members of the wife's family would also be present.

Tibbles met me at the door, thanked me for coming, and led me into the stillness of the empty house. We were alone. For some time we sat silent together in the front room. At length he arose, saying, "I think you have never met her. Shall we go and see her now?" Taking my hand again, he led me into the adjoining bedroom.

There was no coffin, as I remember. I see her lying on the bed, her body covered by a sheet, her hands resting on her breast, a wet cloth folded across her face. Having removed the cloth, Tibbles stood for a while with head bowed above the waxen face, his shoulders shaking as with a chill.

"Isn't she beautiful?" he said with tears running down his cheeks; and truly, in a seeming afterglow of death, strange beauty lingered on the ageless face. I remember thinking how pretty she must have been in the heyday of Indian girlhood when Tibbles first saw her. And how grand a figure he must have been to her—a lion of a man, with flowing locks, bushy brows, and noble mien. For Tibbles looked somewhat as our statesmen used to look in steel engravings, save for several unpleasantly prominent front teeth.

Having rinsed the cloth in a pail of cold well water, he wrung it out and folded it gently across her face. Then we returned to the front room.

After we had sat awhile in silence, Tibbles began to talk, as though he had forgotten what was waiting —but not for him—in the still room yonder.

More than half a century later, some years after Tibbles died, the long lost manuscript of his memoirs was discovered and published under the title *Buckskin and Blanket Days*. Much of it was a twice-told tale for me, as I had heard it from the lips of Tibbles himself during that weird night of bittersweet remembering: his experiences as a youth living with the Omaha tribe; his brief association with old John Brown in Kansas; the tragic removal of the Poncas to the Indian Territory—nothing less than the crucifixion of a people; old Chief Standing Bear's long, desperate journey, bringing the dead body of his son back to the land of his fathers for burial; the famous trial and epoch-making decision of Judge Dundy, proclaiming an Indian "a person" in the meaning of the law. And then the valiant, glorious years when he and she worked together for Indian rights! It was a holding tale, and, like Aeneas of old, always the teller was a part of his story.

Several times during the creeping hours of that vigil he returned to the hushed room to change the cloth upon the dear dead face and weep.

Once when the night was getting old and he had grown garrulous with weariness and the lapse of sorrow, he recalled an anecdote of General Crook. Having been invited to speak before the Indian Rights Society in Boston, the general had come all the way from the western plains to deliver one of the shortest and most effective speeches ever to fall from the lips of a man: "Ladies and Gentlemen," so, according to Tibbles, ran the speech, "I have been fighting Indians in the West for twenty-five years. During that time I have never known an Indian to break a treaty. I have never known a white man to keep one! I thank you."

Tibbles, overcome by his yarn, was seized by a spasm of explosive laughter. Part nasal nicker and high-pitched whinny, part raucous bray, the desecrating racket smote the mournful stillness of the house, to cease abruptly as he realized again what waited yonder.

Then I must have fallen asleep, for presently I was aware of sudden dawn abroad in the world and Tibbles snoring in his chair.

10.

Big Payment Days

Aside from the purchasing of good heirship lands at prices often absurdly low, short-term money lending was the most profitable "Indian business." The proceeds from heirship land sales were paid out to the sellers through the government office at the reservation agency on certain big payment days, and there was much borrowing against the impatiently awaited carnivals of cash.

For instance, an Indian would borrow twenty-five dollars, giving his note (wah-bug-a-zee, I believe) for thirty-five or more in respectful acknowledgment of a white man's mystery known as "intress." The formidable document would be duly thumb marked (if the victim couldn't write), impressively stamped in the presence of the customer, and most likely "secured" by mortgage on a team and wagon already heavily encumbered. The note would become payable a month or two later when the next flood of crisp paper money began to flow.

According to a ruling of the Indian Bureau in Washington, no collector would be allowed nearer than thirty rods from the pay station while a big payment was in progress. Accordingly there was an established taw line, as it were, along which the human buzzards hovered, ready to swoop down on the prey when the names of debtors were bawled out by the bull-lunged criers at the station door. (Du-ba-

mun-na!) Sometimes a collector, hearing the name of a particularly slippery client, would take off into the brush in hot pursuit of the fleeing debtor, intent upon waylaying him while his supply of cash was still unravished by greedy creditors.

While waiting along the taw line and listening to the criers, we passed the time by pitching horseshoes, practicing leapfrog, playing mumblety-peg with jackknives, spinning yarns, shooting craps, or taking a hand at poker, several games of which were generally underway on spread-out horse blankets. Poker was a prime source of profit for my boss, who had a mean way with a pack of cards and could pick a straight flush right out of the air, it was said. He usually came home from a big payment with a comfortable roll, which I was instructed to enter in the cashbook with the facetious notation, "Agency deals." That little witticism became standard in our office and always rated a chuckle. Agency deals!

The collection of doubtful accounts offered no serious problem to those favored ones who belonged to the right group and had a friendly understanding with the major. Such were admitted into the pay station by the back door, and the cashing of a note was thus made to seem an official government transaction, not to be questioned.

11.

Mister Cabney

It was during my employment in the office of J. J. Elkin that I became acquainted with Antoine Cabanné.

"Mister Cabney," as we called him, was something of a town character, often addressed with just a touch of restrained amusement and a slightly overdone show of respect. He was short legged, long armed, and heavy shouldered, with hands notably large and sinewy.

In the early years of our century when he and I became good friends, he would have been well along in his seventies, or maybe even his eighties, although his coarse black hair, bristling low on his forehead, was only thinly sifted with gray, and he had not yet begun to shuffle as he walked. He had, however, as I clearly recall, begun to bend forward a trifle in his going, as though to lean a little against a freshening wind of years. But his dark-skinned, craggy face told more of race and weather than of age.

Mister Cabney was the son of Jean P. Cabanné, a French aristocrat of St. Louis, then prominent in the Missouri River fur trade. His mother was an Omaha Indian woman. It was his proud boast, often repeated, that he was "the first white child born in Nebraska," although he scarcely looked the part. That there was no disgrace in this situation is indicated by the fact that the boy was taken to St.

Louis by his father for a visit with his white relatives there. The extended saga of the downstream voyage on a raft, and a wild Indian boy's experiences in the big village, was an important one in the old man's repertory.

Although he had failed to penetrate the mysteries of writing and reading, he was unquestionably a star pupil in his study of good manners. I think I have never, in a long life, known any other man quite so polite as Mister Cabney. He always called me "Sir" and sat with uncovered head when he talked with me in my office. If, in walking on the street, he chanced to meet a lady whom he knew (and apparently every woman was a lady in his eyes), he stopped, bowed low from the hips, and the downward flourish of his hat almost swept the sidewalk.

Having nothing else to do but to remember yesterday and wait with patience for tomorrow, Mister Cabney, by long habit, had established a definite succession of vantage points from which to view the passing world. Weather and season permitting, he was sure to be seen daily, at a given place, at a given time, ready for the loan of any receptive ear. A favored spot, after the sun began its westward slant and shadows lengthened, was the front porch of the hotel with its hospitable chairs for loungers.

The old man's "tall tales," as they might well have seemed, must have been most amusing to the incredulous traveling men from the city—tall indeed, and even taller in reality than a "city slicker" might imagine. For there were those who had taken the trouble to check the old man's yarns against history and contemporaneous accounts to learn how exact the cherished memories of a wholly unlettered man might be. I had come to the conclusion that the simple story of his life was essentially the history of the great Missouri River steamboat era in its heyday. From cabin boy and deckhand to engineer, he knew the river, bend by bend from St. Louis to Fort Benton, Montana—more than two thousand miles.

In unfriendly weather he was likely to be found in my office, if the coast was clear, or in his favorite chair at the barbershop. He would enter the shop briskly and make directly for the shoeshine section, probably by way of justifying the visit. Juri, the barber, with his puckish sense of fun, would sometimes lower his tonsorial chair and get busy preparing his towels as for a prospective customer, inquiring solicitously of the visitor, "Shave, Mister?" This cryptic witticism was good for a snicker or two among the lounging audience, for it was plain to see that Mister Cabney had been stingily endowed with the Indian's wispy token of whiskers.

I think he was particularly happy there, where bright young blades of the village congregated at times for rowdy clowning and boisterous merrymaking. How good it was to be young! And what polite interest they showed in his reminiscences!

"Mister Cabney, do you remember the old *Silver Heels?*"

Whereupon he was off again.

"Yes, yes, the *Silver Heels!* I mind her well! A sidewheeler, and as pretty a boat as ever floated." Then he would tell who built her and when and where, and who the captain was, and where she sank.

But it is not to be supposed that the fate of the *Silver Heels* or any other ill-starred craft would necessarily conclude the old man's yarn, for there were hundreds of steamboats plying the river in his better days. Some four hundred of them ended in disaster, making the treacherous stream a long graveyard of boats. Mister Cabney knew scores upon scores of them by name (a truly Homeric catalog of ships); and the fate of one led him to the fate of others. If one was ripped open by a concealed snag, he was reminded of another that went down in flames, or another destroyed by the explosion of overheated steam boilers in some desperate encounter with fast water or bucking the wind around some gusty headland. And so on and on, until perhaps he became uncomfortably conscious of chairs gone empty.

"Please sit down, Mr. Neihardt, and await further orders from me. I have much to tell you." And indeed he did have much to tell, as I was to learn in the next few days. First of all, he wanted to tell about the story of his long, adventurous life that had been written by a young St. Louis author, Joseph Mills Hanson. Several "well-posted" people, I was assured, had read and liked the manuscript. But a number of eastern publishers had rejected it—perhaps the company I represented would be interested.

At this point the appearance of Captain Gould on the hurricane deck ended our interview. "Mr. Neihardt, would you please help the boys with the lumber yonder?" And so I did, proceeding up the gangplank at a dogtrot, like a well-trained and ambitious roustabout. When I returned aboard with a scantling balanced on either shoulder, I passed Captain Gould, and he grinned pleasantly at me. I worked faithfully all forenoon save for an occasional breathing spell when Marsh commanded me to "come sit down, please, Mr. Neihardt."

When dinner was announced by the cook banging merrily upon his frying pan with a ladle, I learned what the pleasant grin had signified. A table had been set in the drafty shade of the lower deck and spread with a red-and-white-checkered cloth for elegance. After I had sloshed face and hands in a bucket of river water, I was headed for the galley, where the crew was already busy feeding, when Gould tapped me on the shoulder and motioned me toward an empty chair at the table reserved for "the quality." Evidently the fine line of social cleavage on the *Expansion* excluded all below the rank of engineer. Sitting there, I might well have been mistaken for a mate or an assistant pilot.

During the long days while the *Expansion* rooted and groaned her way among the snags and bars like a giant pig, it was my privilege to share the high and windy pilothouse with Marsh as he handled the great pilot wheel.

In the first white of daybreak the *Expansion* backed out of her moorings, idled a short way down the Missouri to the junction of the rivers, and, with panting engines and pluming stacks, swung out into the tawny current of the Yellowstone. Far bluffs heard her bellowing of farewell and answered mournfully.

Marsh had invited me to be with him in the pilot-house, happily with no objection from Gould. As we rounded the tongue of land where the two rivers merged and the wide landscape broke out before me, I remembered how much had happened there, at the wedding of the waters, before time changed the world.

Where our camp stood was the site of old Fort Union, a fabulous establishment in its heyday of the 1830s. There the reigning bourgeois, Alexander Mackenzie, dominated a vast fur-trade empire, being known as "the king of the upper Missouri." There Maximilian, prince of Wied-Neu-Wied, spent a part of a winter with old Hugh Glass, then already a legend around the campfires of the West. Hugh, we are told, dictated to the prince the story of his amazing life and adventures. Within a few miles from where the steamer was fighting her way against the stubborn current, Hugh Glass, in the winter of 1832, was finally run to earth by his old enemies, the Rees.

How many masted keelboats, laden with goods for the Indian trade and engined with men, had come that way! Yonder on the tongue of land between the two rivers Ashley-Henry men had built a fort in the fall of 1822. Within view of the *Expansion*'s pilot-house would be the place of Carpenter's tragic death. Had not steamboats by the hundreds filled the lonely river reaches with their raucous voices on their way to Benton—and oblivion?

It was the time of falling water, and the pilot's problems increased daily. The *Mandan* had ascended the river when the crest of the June rise was already passing, and she left Benton for the return voyage to St. Louis as soon as possible. We, on the contrary, had lingered at Benton until the middle of August, completing our boat. All through the laggard hours of the late summer day I watched the skillful handling of the craft, dodging bars and snags, bucking capricious crosscurrents in patches of fast water. Now and then she shivered to an abrupt stop, her engine bell jangling, and backed up to make a fresh attempt, breathing like an asthmatic giant. However, the situation was excellent for the occasional lessons in pilotage the captain was giving me—pointing out signs of deep and shallow water, how to follow the angling channel by studying the far shore.

At several lonely landings we nosed the boat's prow into the bank, pausing to deliver some small consignment of freight, and at such times I renewed my status as a deckhand by responding to the polite invitation from Captain Gould to "work." Will you please carry this or that up the bank? And I did.

Once, after a prolonged silence, Captain Marsh turned to me with a far-away look and said: "Thirty-two years ago this last Fourth of July, I brought the old *Far West* along here, running like a scared jackrabbit. I had a cargo of pain and misery—the wounded men from Reno's battalion. We had them bedded down on two feet of slough grass cut in the swampy lands along the river—two decks full of them. Orders were to get the suffering men from Terry's headquarters at the mouth of the Little Bighorn to Fort Abraham Lincoln as quickly as possible, a distance of seven hundred and ten miles. The *Far West* made it in fifty-six hours. It was said we made the fastest trip ever made by a Missouri riverboat. Surely it was one of the wildest! It frightens me yet to think of the chances we took, for we ignored all obstacles and plunged on, day and night. We knew better, but something was driving me and the old *Far West*. The hazards only made her seem to come alive. At times, I swear, there were other hands on that wheel. I could feel them.

"But we carried more than suffering men. We carried the terrible, widow-making news of Custer's massacre."

Thereupon, still reading the river ahead with narrowed gaze and occasionally spinning the great wheel, he recalled stirring incidents of the Sioux War in 1876 in the Yellowstone country. The *Far West* had been chartered by the government and detailed to operate with General Terry's forces north of the river to transport troops and supplies. I saw through the captain's brooding eyes Custer and the Seventh riding away from Gibbon's headquarters at the mouth of the Rosebud into the realm of no return.

In obedience to Gibbon's orders Captain Marsh had managed to take the *Far West* to the mouth of the Little Bighorn. There he was to meet General Terry, who was sorely in need of supplies. It had been a well-nigh impossible feat—a steamboat cruising the

There followed a period of anxiety, with regular visits to the post office at mail time. Although I knew I was unreasonable in expecting a reply so soon, I was always there just the same, watching like a mousing cat, as the letters fell into the boxes. Maybe the next one would be mine!

I have previously mentioned my theory of dynamic cosmic patterns.

Although I could not know it then, I was about to be caught up into the pattern of the Indian consciousness. It was a new pattern in my experience that, in large measure, was to condition my thinking and feeling about the world the remainder of my life.

As I stood there one day eagerly mousing my mailbox, a Mr. J. J. Elkin, an Indian trader whom I knew well, asked me what I was doing. I told him I was doing some free-lance writing. He wondered if I would care to help him in his office. I would, especially as he assured me there would be time on the job when I could write.

I agreed to work for Mr. Elkin for thirty dollars a month as stenographer, bookkeeper, collector, and maker of maps showing Indian allotments.

Shortly after making the agreement with Mr. Elkin I did receive an acceptance for "The Tiger's Lust" with a check for twenty-five dollars. It was just enough to pay for my mother's false teeth.

Heirship lands had recently been released by the government for sale to the highest bidder, and, accordingly, easy money was flowing through the pockets of the notably improvident Indians. A rank money smell was abroad in the land, and money-hungry white sons of civilization flocked about the reservation like buzzards about a rotting carcass.

Business was good indeed, as indicated by the following snatch of characteristic conversation between my boss and a landowner.

My boss: "Say, Tom, how much an acre do you folks want for your Grandpa's quarter section?"

The landowning heir (importantly): "Well, now, Misser Elkin, we talk a long time about this. Then we say we guess we ask you twenty dollah. You no give us twenty, then we take ten or maybe fifteen, if you give it to us."

Obviously this was a long way from what I have called *cosmic patterns.* It was, in fact, merely one of many indications of what some of the younger Indians were becoming under the benign influence of civilization.

And here I am reminded of another episode of similar general import, although it has no bearing on the price of land. It is, rather, about the price of coffins (of all things) and a certain mixed blood by the name of Fred Leman.

Fred was an amiable, soft-spoken soul, with a singular gift of persuasion. Otherwise he was distinguished by an outsize thirst for strong drink that was always on the prowl for further refreshment.

On the midsummer day I now have in mind, Fred was headed for town with his rattletrap spring wagon and crowbait team. It was cruelly hot on the dusty reservation road and Fred was thirsty. He was getting thirstier by the mile, and he was thinking hard, we may be sure, for he was entirely without funds. I suspect he was thinking fondly of me and the possibility of floating yet another small loan from me—say fifty cents or maybe a "dollah." He still owed me for the last flotation and still does; but he has long since been gathered to his fathers. May he rest in peace!

Several miles from town Fred came abreast of a little tumbledown shack squatting in hopeless squalor by the side of the road. It was full of mourning voices—*wahoo-ha-a-a*—and the bitter wailing of children.

Evidently somebody had died in there; and, being curious, as well as wishing to be helpful perhaps, Fred tied his team to the hitching post and entered the house of sorrow. I wasn't there, of course, but I knew Fred and was familiar with the tales floating about the incident, so I may venture to reconstruct the affair.

I can see the recently deceased, still sprawled in indecent abandon across the bed of death, as when the final agony seized him. I can see the sagging jaw, the stare of unlidded eyes, the frozen look of blank astonishment.

I see Fred, all sympathy and bustling competence, taking charge of the sad situation like a good Samaritan. They were going to need a coffin in that house right away, and Fred had an inspiration. He knew the family had recently received money at the big payment. His team was already harnessed and hitched. He himself would fetch the coffin; and, because he felt so sorry, he would charge only five "dollahs" for a fine one! No doubt Fred's exceptional gift of plausibility, aided by the shock of grief, readily completed the melancholy business; and Fred was off on his mission of mercy.

People living along the reservation road to town used to tell with gusto, and perhaps some artistic exaggeration, the tale of Fred's wild dash for the undertaking parlor that momentous day—the skin-rack horses beaten into a stumbling lope, the rolling dust cloud with Fred bouncing therein, and plying the goad!

In our town those days, undertaking was a function of the furniture trade; and when Fred entered the establishment, it must have been clear from his disconsolate mien and manner that the next customer was not in the market for furniture.

The following version of the ensuing conversation is adapted from the popular account at the time.

"Old Man Rain Walker all time dead," said Fred in response to the proprietor's anxious question. "All time dead. Two more days, put 'im in the ground."

"What!" exclaimed the proprietor, who knew and liked the Old Man, "You don't mean to say your father-in-law, Rain Walker, is dead!"

"Yeh," Fred replied. "He get awful sick in his belly and go dead. Two more days, put 'im in the ground. I come after coffin for the poor Old Man, a real nice one, please. His old woman she say she give you the money when she sell her land." Hereupon, some say, Fred rubbed out a hypothetical tear or two with either fist and fetched a groaning sob.

There followed another wild dash—back to the house of sorrow with the real nice coffin. And soon thereafter still another dash for town—and a friendly bootlegger.

The oft-told tale, in its classic form, has a highly dramatic denouement. The scene is the furniture store. The time is some weeks after the Old Man's untimely and temporary demise. He now enters, hale, hearty, and in what used to be called "high dudgeon."

Old Man Rain Walker (shaking his fist in the proprietor's face and shouting): "Next time I die I come get my own coffin!"

Curtain.

I once played a scurvy trick on Fred; and with a contrite heart I now seize this belated opportunity to confess and so perhaps make amends to a kindly soul. It was like this:

The office where I held forth was a short block from the railway station. One day, just at train time, Fred bustled into my presence all out of breath with a sad story, about as follows:

"My wife, she awful sick, Missa Naha, and she need some medicine or maybe she fall over dead. My team down in Lyons, Missa Naha, and you please lend me twenty-five cents so I buy a ticket to Lyons and get my team. My poor wife awful sick and she no get the medicine maybe she just roll over dead."

Lyons was the next town down the railway, ten miles distant.

Now it just happened that I had seen Fred's unmistakable crowbaits that very afternoon within the hour. They were moping drowsily, and quite hayless, at a hitching rack several blocks up the street.

At this moment the approaching train to Lyons whistled at the edge of town. It gave me a great idea.

"Come on, Fred!" I yelled, feeling the need of excitement for my purpose. "There's your train for Lyons. Come quick! Come quick! They don't wait long. Hurry! Hurry!"

I hustled him through the office door into the street and began herding him toward the railway station, occasionally giving him an encouraging "bum's rush." My brisk surprise attack, together with my excited shouting, seemed to render Fred practically helpless. And, anyway, hadn't he begged piteously for a trip to Lyons?

We reached the station as the locomotive clanked and panted to a stop. I hustled Fred aboard, gave him a quarter for the conductor in lieu of a ticket, and swung off the car as it set out again for Lyons.

I must confess it still gives me a twinge of remorse to recall the incredulous, hurt look of consternation on Fred's face as he leaned out the car window looking helplessly back at me.

That evening I took Fred's team to a livery stable for a square meal and a drink.

When I next saw Fred he was the same soft-spoken, gentle soul as ever. I never knew how he got back to Bancroft, and I never had the nerve to inquire.

We soon dropped the painful subject. He suggested that I might like to go with him on the *Expansion* next trip up the Yellowstone. Perhaps I could find some material for my *Outing* articles, and he could teach me something about reading water and following the channel by cutbanks. I would have to get Captain Gould's permission. So I broached the matter to Gould at once and was told gruffly that the *Expansion* was no excursion boat and he didn't want any "condemned" passenger messing around on board with a camera. But on second thought, he could use another roustabout to help in loading cargo. Was I afraid of work? he inquired. If not, I could come along but, by god, I'd have to work! I had been observing the deckhands at their alleged labors, and I remarked to Gould, if that was what he called work, I was sure I could qualify. So, leaving my party in charge of our riverside camp to await my return from upriver, I joined the *Expansion* crew and began to "work." But I soon noted that I worked only when Captain Gould was present or plainly visible in the offing. For it was clear that Captain Marsh had wanted to take me along as a guest and was disgusted by the brusque treatment I had received.

We were taking on a cargo of lumber, and I was happily thrilled to share in the operation, which was pure romance to me. Serving as deckhand on the Yellowstone with the famous Captain Marsh! Think of it!

He was sitting on a bench at the foot of the companionway watching the dedicated sons of labor at their leisurely devotions. I was making for another load when he ordered me to "come sit down, please, Mr. Neihardt." Of course I came. "But Captain," I objected, dreading another encounter with Gould, "I came aboard to work."

Marsh was employed as her master and pilot. As I approached, he came out of the pilothouse and called down to me in that wind-like voice of his: "I saw you at Benton—come aboard." Obviously he was used to having his commands obeyed without delay, and I went forthwith.

Although eighty-three years old and a bit stout about the waist, in keeping with his years, he still walked erect—over six feet of him, I judged. By the spread of his shoulders he had been, and probably still was, a man of unusual physical strength. There was a brooding, long-focused look in his eyes that accented the suggestion of a hawk-peaked nose.

Seated in the shadow of the pilothouse, we were soon talking about my proposed descent of the river. He was most encouraging. "Don't let them scare you," he said, "You will learn to judge the water and follow the channel by watching the cutbanks. Just don't drift at night. I started at the age of eight as cabin boy on the Ohio River. That was seventy-five years ago, and although my hull needs some repairs, I am still afloat."

It was good to be back on the Yellowstone again, he remarked during a pause in our conversation. It was especially good to get away from St. Louis, where, it appeared, there had been some altercation with the law. Answering my question as to the nature of the disagreement, he replied, "They said in court that I almost killed a man."

"But did you?" I urged.

"Well," he replied, "it was a little matter in a restaurant on the St. Louis riverfront. Some words were passed and I hit him on the head with a sugar bowl. I'll have no man speak ill of my blessed mother—rest her soul."

had been employed to guide the government boat on her maiden voyage from Mondak to Benton and back.

The master of the *Mandan* looked me over curiously with what I took to be an amused, if not a deprecating, smile. "So you are the fellow who is going down this river," he said. I admitted the allegation. He said, "Well, you'll never make it." "Why?" I asked. "Isn't there water enough?" "Yes," he replied, "but you won't find it."

And I almost didn't.

Fifteen hundred miles downstream and nearly two months later I met the *Mandan* again. She was snorting and churning her way upstream across the bar at the mouth of Cherry Creek. I had my moment of triumph by hailing her master. "I found that water," I shouted. He came out of his lofty pilothouse and greeted me with friendly laughter and the prizefighter's two-fisted gesture of victory.

My next meeting with Marsh was on the riverfront at Mondak near the Yellowstone's mouth. He had left Benton some weeks before we had and returned with the *Mandan* as far as Mondak. We were just completing the most difficult portion of our voyage, six hundred miles and thirty rapids below Benton. Half naked and sun blackened from swimming with the towline, I steered around a sharp, left-hand, timbered bend and came suddenly upon the *Expansion,* riding sleepily at her moorings. She was engaged in freighting supplies from the railroad at Mondak to the Crane Creek Irrigation Project, which was then under construction and several days by boat up the Yellowstone, and she was taking on her next cargo.

12.

Captain Marsh

It was in August 1908 that I met Capt. Grant P. Marsh, the veteran steamboat pilot of the Missouri River. I had contracted with Casper Whitney, editor of *The Outing Magazine,* to descend the Missouri River in my own open boat and to write a series of eight articles on my experiences in that adventure.

I was camped with my photographer and a boy companion on a gravel bar across the river from Fort Benton, Montana, the head of Missouri River navigation. We were busy building our boat for the voyage when a new government snag boat, the *Mandan,* arrived from St. Louis, more than two thousand miles downstream. She was truly a beautiful craft, built largely of steel and thoroughly equipped for lifting snags out of the river. She was the first steamboat in eighteen years to reach Fort Benton. Also, I believe, she was the last. And when I followed her, I wondered how she ever managed to make her way to the top of that long, watery stairway.

Shortly after her arrival we received a note brought to us by a deckhand of the *Mandan,* inviting us to come and see them. I went and found three captains waiting for me on the hurricane deck. In addition to the boat's master there was a Captain Gould, one of the owners of the steamer *Expansion,* then operating on the lower Yellowstone; and there was the famous veteran pilot, Grant P. Marsh, who

5.

Back Home in Bancroft

Emboldened by my success with the "Song of the Turbine Wheel," I mailed my "Lonesome in Town" to *The Youth's Companion*. I now gave myself over, heart and soul, to the completion of my prose tale, "The Tiger's Lust."

Before my Omaha adventure I had partially conceived the plot, with no less a personage than the great Mogul Shah Jahan himself as the principal character. Several evenings had been spent in research at the Omaha Public Library, which left me with ample ignorance for the free play of creative imagination.

Also I had examined several copies of the *Ledger* by way of acquainting myself with its literary flavor. It has been more than three-score years and ten since I last set eyes upon that masterpiece and I have only the vaguest memories of it, as a whole. I do recall something about bulbuls singing in a moonlit garden, and I don't know why. But I definitely remember the final sentence of the tragic tale. It read: "And she never smiled again!"

When at length winter struck in earnest, with occasional spells of sub-zero weather, my attic room was no place for bulbuls, real or imagined; and before Christmas I was at home in Bancroft, continuing to work on my story. "The Tiger's Lust" was completed in early Februrary and sent at once to the editors of the *Ledger*.

his divinely condemned money. Whereupon I withdrew to my attic.

That afternoon there was a sign in the café window. Next day it was gone, and the incident was closed.

round about that a naughty story had just been un-corked. Immediately thereafter the sudden silence that fell about the table made it clear that the scrub-man with his mop and bucket had been sighted and recognized. Then followed what I have since come to regard as a comedy of embarrassments—they, ap-parently indulging a barefaced make-believe that I wasn't really there at all—and I, wishing to goodness it were so. Meanwhile I was vigorously plying the mop as though I were giving some corrupt city gov-ernment what it surely needed. No doubt, I was making little progress, being more concerned with the embarrassing predicament than with the work at hand.

At this point my boss arrived on the scene, evi-dently to inspect the job. Perhaps he got out of bed on the wrong side that morning, or perhaps I was at fault. Howsoever, he proceeded to give me what is known in the vernacular as a good "bawling out." Considering that my pride was already raw sore, his remarks were like throwing salt into an open wound.

I grant I was undignified, even impolite, and I mention the affair only because I wish to be faithful to my obligation as an accurate historian. The hair crawled upon the back of my neck, and I recall telling him precisely where to go straight to and what to do with his sloppy mop pail when he got there. Then, having violently sloshed the mop into the bucket, I headed for the door.

"Stop and get your pay," my boss shouted after me.

By this time I must have been enjoying my indig-nation, for, assuming a noble attitude, I shouted back that I would be no man's slave and I wanted none of

Then I would scrub the dining-room floor and place the chairs and tables in order. The remainder of the twenty-four hours would be mine, but I would be subject to call in cases of emergency. I would have my meals in the kitchen and would receive a salary of three dollars a week. It was a good arrangement for my purpose, and I proceeded to make the most of it.

With my modest terminal pay received from the *Daily News* I was able to buy some needed stationery and rent an old double keyboard Smith-Premier. It was like mine at home. Somehow it increased my confidence. Thus I was definitely in business as a man of letters.

And lo and behold! I did receive a letter of acceptance from *The Youth's Companion* for my "Song of the Turbine Wheel." It contained a crisp, expensive-looking check that read "Fifteen and 50/100 dollars" —not bad for thirty-one lines, and real money, good anywhere. Evidently my luck was changing for the better; and just let those editors wait until they saw my "Lonesome in Town"—especially the first stanza! I was almost willing to bet they would pay a dollar a line.

One day during the noon hour I was sent into the dining room with a bucket of water and a mop to finish cleaning the floor where some nervous waitress had crashed a loaded tray. As I approached the scene of petty disaster, I became uncomfortably aware of four men sitting at a nearby table. Three of them I knew as former colleagues on the *Daily News,* who no doubt had witnessed my shameful undoing. The other was a stranger who may have replaced me at city hall, as I surmised. I judged by an explosive outburst of merriment and anxious glances cast open prairies in search of a river! Often he was obliged to use the steam capstan to haul the boat over shallows and rapids, or to have her crew drag her from water hole to water hole.

But had he not been known to boast: "Yes I can take her out on dry land if there has been a heavy dew the night before"?

The *Far West* had finally reached her destination on the twenty-fifth of June. She was tied up at an island in the middle of the river opposite the mouth of the Little Bighorn, as a precaution against Indian attack.

Early in the morning of the twenty-sixth an Indian broke through the thick willow brush at the junction of the two rivers. He was tearing his hair and wailing mournfully. Captain Marsh and several of the officers were astonished to recognize him as Curley, one of Custer's Crow scouts. He was taken aboard the steamer and, since he understood no English, one of the officers gave him a pencil and paper, indicating that he should draw a picture of what had happened.

Sitting down in front of the medicine chest on the foredeck, Curley drew a small circle of dots on the paper, wailing the while, and saying "absoraka, absoraka, absoraka (our people)" with each jab of the pencil. Making a larger circle enclosing the smaller one, he rapidly placed many dots between the inner and outer circles, saying as he did so, "Sioux, Sioux, Sioux, Sioux." Then with upraised arms accented by a forward thrust of his whole body, he indicated the outcome: "Pouf!"

It was clear to Captain Marsh that our troops had met with disaster.

The foregoing is the story told me by Captain Marsh on the Yellowstone in 1908. Nine years later, in 1917, I was lecturing in colleges and universities on the West Coast. I had heard that Curley was living at the Crow Indian Agency in Montana. So I decided to visit him on my return trip East, which I did, spending three days with him.

Curley had the reputation among those who did not know him well of being one of the biggest liars in the West. Upon becoming better acquainted with him, I understood how he had won this distinction. He had an enormous sense of humor and he delighted in concocting fabulous tales for credulous journalists, in which he was generally the hero. (As I say this, I can see the crow's feet of curious innocence crinkling about his mock-serious eyes.) Curley's attitude toward me changed abruptly when he learned that Captain Marsh and I were actually friends.

The Custer Battlefield is only a short distance from the Crow Indian Agency; and Curley and I and an interpreter decided to visit it—horseback—and revive old memories. As we entered the Battlefield a rheumy-eyed old man was cutting brush along a rutted road leading up to the iron-fenced monument. He looked up at me with a veiled stare and asked slowly, "Are—you—Captain—'So and So'?"

I wasn't; and I suspect that his captain had long since fought his last battle alone. Perhaps there was some suggestion of the military about my general appearance. I was wearing a black overcoat with padded shoulders, and I was riding a white horse.

Scattered over the hilltop and the slope to the river were many wooden headboards, silently repeating the tragic tale.

It was February and ice jams on the Little Bighorn were being dynamited. "Boom, boom!" said Curley, "Big fight—all same! Heap big fight."

"Curley," I said, "will you tell us what you did in that big fight here on the hill?" The following is substantially the answer I received:

"There were three of us Crow boys and an interpreter in the advance with Long Hair (Custer). When we came to that ridge over there, Long Hair called us Crow boys to him and said: 'I did not pay you to fight. I paid you to show me the enemy and you have done it—now save yourselves.' He gave me a paper with writing on it and told me to take it to that man over there (Reno?) and hurry! The two other boys ran away at once and turned up with Terry's forces a few days later."

"And what did you do?" I asked.

"I started to obey the order but when I got to that gulch yonder, it was full of Sioux and Cheyenne warriors and I couldn't get across. When I got on this hill over here (pointing), I could see that Long Hair was already fighting hard and he was going to get rubbed out. I was only sixteen, never been to war before, and I thought it was a pretty good time to run."

"Where did you go?" I urged.

"I ran out into the hills—away from the fighting —and I cried all night, because I would never see Long Hair again."

My visit at the agency had ended. My good-byes had been said to Curley and his friends. I was already at the depot, pacing up and down the platform, waiting for the evening train to take me away.

Loud shouting roused me from my musing over my recent happy experiences. I looked up and saw Curley and the interpreter coming down the wooden sidewalk, waving wildly as they came. I wondered what I was in for now! The interpreter approached me and said, "Curley—he think about you." I said, "Yes, and you may tell him that I think about him too, and it makes me glad."

The interpreter said, "Curley say he wants you to be his brother-friend until he dies, so that if he get into trouble you tell him what to do."

Curley fixed me with an expectant gaze, searching my face for his answer. Again the interpreter spoke: "And Curley, he say he wants you to take his ring and wear it, so that when you look at it, you think of him."

The ring was a sad affair, judged by jeweler's standards. It was undeniably solid brass, and in lieu of a gem setting it bore the image of a hostile lion's head. The eyes were purest red glass.

Removing the ring from his little finger, Curley placed it on my ring finger. Whereupon I said: "I take his ring and will be his brother-friend until I die." Then I gave him a ring from my hand that had been given to me by southwestern Indians. He took it; and it was a tight fit on his little finger. "Ah-h, ah-h-h, ah-h-h," he said, shaking my hand vigorously.

The clanking arrival and exhausting steam of the locomotive ended our talk. After a brief pause the one passenger to be picked up was "all aboard" with his baggage.

The train was moving out of the yards at a steadily increasing speed. I opened the coach window and looked back. Curley was standing where I had left him, waving his arms above his head. I watched until he disappeared in the distance. I was not to see him again in this life.

13.

An Overnight Journey

It was in the early summer of 1907 that I first met my dog friend, Shep. Sixty years thereafter we had another memorable meeting.

Or did we?

That is the story I want to tell, for what it may be worth, to those who do not know as yet quite all the answers. As for the others, the lazy word *coincidence* will do.

I was vacationing with my mother and sister in Spearfish Canyon of the Black Hills, seriously practicing the fine art of fly casting. Our cabin stood close beside lovely Little Spearfish Creek, some twenty yards above a cataract where the happy crystal waters thundered into the Big Spearfish sixty feet below, straight down. It was right there in our front yard, day in, day out, the deep-bass hallelujah chorus singing glory.

Not more than eight or ten feet from our front door ran the track of the Deadwood-Spearfish railway. About a hundred yards downgrade, toward the terminal town of Spearfish, was a pausing place for the little mountain train. Officially known as Savoy, it consisted visibly of three cabins, counting ours. Otherwise it was built of awe. Awe indeed and awe in plenty, with the brooding pine-clad summits and the bald peaks round about; the rock wall yonder soaring a dizzy thousand feet or more above the valley; the plunging trout stream at its base, filling the resonating hollow of the canyon with its ceaseless intoning.

But this was long ago in the pristine days before the great flood wrecked the railway; before scientific progress killed the happy crystal creek; before the cataract quit singing to the sun and moon and stars.

It seems now that people were more human in those days, less occupied with having than with being. Even the little one-car railway train seemed neighborly. Making a leisurely round trip once a day in the busier season, or down one day and back the next when traffic slackened, it never appeared to be pressed for time. Why, it would gladly drop you off anywhere you liked along the brawling stream, or pick you up wherever you might be waiting, done out, perhaps, from wading and casting in the rapids.

Since nothing much often got around to happening in our canyon—mostly day and night and weather—the arrivals of our train never ceased to be events. Having announced its approach with its bull-mouthed, many-echoing whistle, out of all proportion to its size, it was commonly welcomed by most of the meager population. As the little locomotive clanked and panted to a stop with a gusty sigh of satisfaction, one could almost imagine it wearily wiping its headlight and gasping, "My God! I made it! Didn't I?"

And well might it sigh with relief and self-satisfaction, having completed the perilous descent from Englewood into the canyon, for there were frightfully dubious curves (nearly four hundred in thirty miles of track); astonishing spiral grades (twenty-seven hundred vertical feet in twenty-five lineal miles); scores of incredible trestles ingeniously poised over giddy abysses. It was like the fantasy of some inspired engineer on a monumental binge! But it worked, with never an accident; and it was regarded as one of the world wonders of railroad building.

As already noted, our cabin faced the railroad and the soaring rock wall beyond Big Spearfish valley, with our own miniature Niagara in the front yard. There was a large living room for sleeping and cooking and getting in out of the rain if necessary. The lean-to bedroom next to Little Spearfish creek was my own. Up back of me, a matter of a mile or a little less perhaps, a mountain called the Needle's Eye rose boldly above the squatting bluffs along the Little Spearfish. Lying in my bed, I could see it out of my back window, and it had become a fixture in the routine of my days. Being taller than the neighbors, it caught the day far off before any rumor reached the groundlings. Often now it wakened me, and when I saw tomorrow touch the peak, it would be getting on toward time to go a fishing.

Hip booted and fortified with coffee, I would be out in the diluting starlight, drowsy with the voices of the waters, when the dawn glow came seeping in and the landscape stared with morning.

Then began the rainbow battles; and when the sun came up for breakfast, the catch still flopped in the sizzling pan.

It was on such a morning that I had my first memorable meeting with Shep.

I had made my shivering way through the icy dew on the underbrush along the creek and was sitting by a patch of promising water just waiting for the day to broaden a bit.

Suddenly, there he was beside me, wiggling abject

apology for intruding. I recognized him at once. Although we had never met socially, we had occasionally exchanged pleasantries, as one dog to another, on our goings and comings about the canyon. For instance, "How's hunting, old man?" or words of similar import. And maybe there would be a polite reply in "canine tailish"—a most expressive language, by the way, if you can manage the conjugations.

"Well, well," I exclaimed, "and look who's here!"

Apparently he misunderstood my dialect at first, for he groveled before me with a guilty baring of the upper teeth. So I petted him on the head and said, "That's all right, Shep, old man! You may come along and help me fish."

Immediately he was another dog entirely. Intoxicated with joy, he raced wildly about me, around and around, as though pursuing a demented rabbit, yelping with enthusiasm the while.

When at length the spasm of delight was spent and I stooped to pet him, he placed his paws on my shoulders and licked my face. "I'm your dog forever and ever," he said.

And I said, "No, you aren't; you belong to a man up the canyon."

And he said, "No, I am your dog forever because I love you."

And then I said, "Oh well, if it's like that, why of course—." And I began whipping the fast water for a strike while he sat upon his fluffy rump, observing me with tongueful curiosity.

(Dear reader, I know you don't believe a word of this; but you are mistaken. You see, Shep and I had both majored in sentimental linguistics, and we knew how to talk without using silly words. You'd be surprised how much can be said with a slight twitch of the tail or a whisper in the throat. Anyway, he *did* become my dog forever, as this faithful history will relate.)

It was getting quite light by now, and I still can see him as I saw him that morning long ago. Shep was a handsome rascal. A shaggy black mantle, bordered with orange, covered him from the white ring of his nose, across his back, flanks, and haunches to the plume-like white end of his tail. His breast, belly, and knee-length stockings were also white and spotless from frequent cleansing plunges into the pure cold stream.

I must have been casting with a nervous and especially inexpert hand that morning, flicking the line too violently and a split second too soon. At any rate, I threw a gorgeous unhooked rainbow out upon the bank. It looked as though I were about to lose the prettiest fish I'd seen for some time, for it was making back furiously toward the water with flapping leaps and bounds. It was almost there when Shep, seizing the opportunity for a bit of exciting fun, leaped upon the fish, tossed it into the air with his snout, and came down upon it with both front feet, thus blocking escape. So I got my fish.

There was no apologetic behavior from Shep after that. Evidently convinced by praise and petting that he had somehow done a worthy deed for his man, he took on the air of a prosperous partner. While I was casting, he would pace briskly up and down the bank, whimpering with anxiety and eager for action. If a hooked fish broke water in a burst of spinning glory, he would share in the excitement, barking wildly.

It soon became clear that Shep meant to keep me for his man, following me about all day and spending the night on my doorstep. If I tried to shoo him away, he flattened out on his belly and looked utterly forlorn. I thought surely if I didn't feed him he would go home to eat; but food didn't seem to matter. He shadowed me all day, and if any safety barking had to be done at night, he did it thoroughly and as one having authority. When finally I took him to his owner up the canyon, he bolted, making for the brush with a snaky lowering of his head and a desperate drooping of his tail. He did not turn up again until late in the night, when I heard him whining at my back door. He slept that night beside my bed—and many other happy nights thereafter, for by gentleman's agreement he became my dog for the summer.

Soon after this, Shep and I shared an adventure that brought us still closer together. I had received a small bank draft for some verse sold to a New York magazine, and there was no place to cash it short of Deadwood or Spearfish. I had not yet been in the latter town, nor had I seen the canyon below Savoy. So I decided it would be fun to make the fifteen-mile trip on foot downhill to Spearfish and back uphill next morning by the train, which was then running on its alternate-day schedule.

When Shep and I took off together down the railway track, we were as happy as a pair of weanling pups. I was wearing my hobnailed boots that later took me pretty much all over the northern Black Hills. I remember declaring on occasion (perhaps in an exuberant mood) that every time I stepped in them I split a rock and also that they needed nothing but guidance from me. There was a currently popular song with such a burden, and I sang it gaily now to the mocking canyon walls: "I only have to guide 'em and they take me anywheres."

Shep was in a dither of excitement, nosing about among the tangled rumors of a world far larger than previously supposed; and when he yelped in close pursuit of nothing in particular, adjacent gulches filled with ghostly dogs that yammered back at him.

As for me, there was the excitement of grandeur all about me. And there was the excitement of shouting waters in the nearby stream, falling a hundred feet to the mile.

Halfway to Spearfish, the little train overtook us on its trip down. The engineer, evidently recognizing us as citizens of Savoy, slowed down almost to a stop and hailed us with his bull-mouthed whistle, clearly meaning did we want a ride. We didn't and when I gave him the high sign, he whistled merrily again and resumed his former dizzy speed of a dozen miles or so per hour.

Headed downhill with lungs tingling full of mountain air, I had been swinging along with a dreamy, effortless sense of well-being when I became aware that Shep was no longer in evidence. Looking back, I saw him yonder a hundred yards or more in the rear, limping along like an old man favoring his rheumatic joints. When I reached him, he raised a bleeding paw and whined. The sharp ballast between the railway ties had been too much for the soft pads on his feet. He too needed hobnails.

We were still several miles from Spearfish, and Shep was too big to carry. So I helped him down to the creek and bathed his feet in the cold water while he licked my hands and face in gratitude. With frequent rests and bathings we finally reached town.

The only bank was closed for the day, and the train would leave for Deadwood at 8:30 next morning. So we dropped in at one of the saloons, for who but a barber or a bartender would be likely to know the local answers? Business was slack at that hour and the only customer was vocally asleep in his chair, with open mouth and chin on chest. As we entered, the proprietor sprang into action, busily rubbing the polished bar with a towel.

It was not difficult to become acquainted with a stranger in the Black Hills those days, for something of the old romantic prodigality of spirit that free gold seems to engender in a society still lingered there. Even the neighborly little mountain train exemplified the feeling, as we have noted.

How things were up around Savoy, the long, unreasonable walk, the dog's predicament—these served readily for friendly conversation. Soon we were enjoying the hospitality of the house—a sandwich for teetotaler Shep in lieu of a foaming stein.

When we finally got around to the bank draft, the man behind the bar gave the document a rapid look over, shoved it across to me for endorsement, then counted out the stipulated amount in gold coin. In those spacious days in the Hills there was no folding money in circulation and nothing short of silver had any authority. (What, for instance, could one possibly do with a nickel's worth of anything whatever?)

It was easy to arrange with the hotelkeeper for a little-used back room where Shep, being a sick dog, could sleep beside my bed. Next morning we were allowed to ride back uphill to Savoy in the baggage compartment.

Shep and I shared many adventures after that, always avoiding the railway as a route of travel. We liked best the heavily wooded hills and valleys, the dense, towering forest not yet invaded by the lumber industry, where it seemed no man had ever been before. It was thrilling just to stand and listen to nothing in those hushed green twilights. Several times we spent the night in such solitudes, curling up together in a blanket with heaped cedar boughs for a bed.

Usually, our days at home were devoted chiefly to the art of fishing—early in the forenoon and early in the evening.

Along about midsummer our afternoon party took on a third member. It was Bobbie.

Bobbie was a girl—an accident for which she had no apologies and expected no special consideration. By tacit agreement the Canyon had refused to call her Barbara, renaming her for the boy she should have been—and apparently was at heart. Her family was spending the summer in a cabin up-canyon, and we were casually acquainted with them. I had fished a time or two with her father, who had an office in Deadwood and spent his weekends at Savoy.

One afternoon when Shep and I were sitting in front of our cabin, lazily waiting for the shadows of the summits to deepen a bit in the valley, Bobbie came hoppity skip along the railway track with her braids down her back, a creel hanging at her side, and a fly rod over her shoulder. Greeting us gaily, she inquired when we were going fishing and might she go with us. Indeed she might and did. That is how our threesome began, and thereafter it was usually the girl, the dog, and I when the midges began to swarm along the stream and set the rainbows leaping.

Several times during the summer I made the trip by rail to Deadwood, spending the night in town and returning next forenoon. Shep was left behind, being under contract to do all the watching and barking around our cabin. When I went aboard, he protested violently, shouting things at the innocent train that one would grieve to repeat for English ears. All the while he was struggling desperately against the leash, with Bobbie at the other end of it.

Once, after the train, with me in it, was well underway up the canyon, he managed to break loose and took out after the loud-mouthed monster that had stolen his man. The last I saw of him that day, watching from the rear platform, he was loping wearily back yonder, losing slowly and apparently stumbling on his tongue.

Next day he celebrated the miracle of my return with the old ecstatic orgy of delight. But it was clear thereafter that he wanted no truck with the foul beast. Whenever it invaded our private world, he gave it a savagely frank and thoroughly comprehensive barking over.

It was in the mournful waning of August 1907 that I saw Shep for the last time.

Or did I?

That is the story I am telling for those who may still have some vital answers to learn.

The waning days of August were always the saddest of the year for me, ever since boyhood when they meant that I must put on shoes at last and go back to the servitude of school again. I used to think I could feel and see the great change coming, even a week or so before it actually happened. It seemed to be in the constitution of things. Objects long familiar and friendly took on an alien stare, as though I had become an intruder and they wondered who I was. There was a new note, as of petulant grieving, in the wind around the house at night.

Good-bye was in the air for days before we said it to each other. The moaning waters voiced it; the soaring rock wall yonder knew but didn't care. There would be other fishers, other fish, forever and forever.

The dreaded last day came relentless. The valiant little engine panted up from Spearfish with its car and paused obligingly in front of our now forsaken cabin, drawing deep breaths against the spiral climb ahead to Englewood.

The bull-mouthed whistle sounded, filling the canyon with homesick voices of yesterday.

The last I saw of Bobbie and Shep from the rear platform of the coach, they were huddled forlornly together in front of the deserted cabin with her restraining arms about his neck.

It must have been a week or more after I reached my home in Nebraska that the letter came. It was all about Shep, and he was dead. Refusing to remain with his friend Bobbie, he had set himself to watch at the front door of the vacant cabin facing the railroad. He had ignored all cajoling; and when his old master from up the canyon had attempted to take him by force, he had fought like a mad dog. Twice a day, when the hated little train came through, there was the same savage assault on the monster. Then at last the iron beast had won, and Shep was caught under the engine drive wheels. It had happened right there at the front door of the desolate cabin.

The letter closed with an account of our old

friend's burial and the monument of heaped rocks placed above his grave with a headboard reading:

John's Dog.

For sixty years thereafter I did not visit the Black Hills again.

Then in the summer of 1967 it happened that I gave a recital of poetry at Spearfish State College. Knowing of my summer in nearby Spearfish Canyon more than half a century before, friends urged that we make a sentimental journey to Savoy. Accordingly, a party of eight was assembled, including one white-haired old man, and we set out in two cars for yesterday. On the way up to the land of never-never, we stopped for a roadside picnic lunch, and I found occasion to tell the story of my old friend Shep, incidentally describing the handsome fellow that he was when we were boys together.

Although I had been warned against the changes that progress and the jealous years had brought about, I was saddened by what I found. The fabulous railroad was no more, having been wrecked by the great flood of 1935. The trestles and bridges, the ties and rails had been salvaged, and nothing remained but a few grass-grown portions of the railway embankment here and there. Savoy had become a cabin camp with a modern inn.

Big Spearfish Creek was dry, its once happily shouting waters being diverted into tunnels for the generation of electric power.

Spearfish Falls had quite forgotten its hallelujah chorus and sang no more to the sun and moon and stars. It had a job.

The soaring rock wall yonder still faced the flow of time with the old apathetic stare.

Leaving our cars at the inn, our party approached my old cabin by following the brush-grown railroad right-of-way a matter of a hundred yards or so. As we emerged from the final patch of thicket, there it was, a few yards ahead of us. Save for a small lean-to addition at one end and a coat of green paint, there was surprisingly little change, despite the alien gaze it had for me. My lean-to bedroom, bordering the now empty creek bed, still looked out upon the Needle's Eye that had heralded so many glad tomorrows.

In approaching the cabin, we had paused at the point where the railroad used to pass within a few feet of our front door. "This," I remarked to the party, "is where old Shep must have died fighting the engine he hated."

Then suddenly something happened that has left me with some haunting questions. Out of the nearby brush a big handsome shepherd dog charged upon our company, obviously singling me out from the party of eight as the object of his apparently savage attack. The impact of his powerful body staggered me and I was afraid of him until he stood upon his hindlegs, placed his paws upon my shoulders, and proceeded to give my face an affectionate tongue washing.

"It's Shep! It's Shep!" someone exclaimed. And, for a timeless, stretched-out moment, I think I believed.

There was the same black shawl, bordered with orange, covering back and haunches, the snow-white belly, the white feet, the white-ringed nose, the white plume-like tip of the tail. Surely it could have been my Shep but for a trifling matter of sixty years! And when I hugged and kissed his woolly cheeks as of old, he broke away from me, and with little throaty yelps began the old familiar demented-rabbit chase around me and around, as though celebrating with an orgy of delight the miracle of my return from the overnight journey to Deadwood.

The dog could never have seen me before, and his master was astonished at his unusual behavior with a stranger.

Could it be that the love of old Shep for his man had somehow descended through generations of pups?

14.

The Storming of Bancroft

When occasionally I think of my father after all these years, first of all I become aware of a radiant Sunday morning that really never happened. It is, in fact, a composite of various Sabbath mornings when, scrubbed and dressed by my mother as for a gala day, I took my father's forefinger in my fist and followed with neither curious question nor approving comment into the enchanted woodland of Brush Creek, then still well outside of Kansas City.

When that picture begins to fade, most likely there are footsteps growing dimmer in the darkness, and a voice.

But there is another picture that I like better to recall from among the memorabilia of my father, and curiously enough, he is not in the picture at all. I see a country road under the broiling sun of an autumn afternoon. A low dust cloud floating over a half mile of men plodding in rout step—the 22d Regular Infantry.

That was the day I joined up unofficially and became a veteran buddy of his buddies. It is a story that I like to tell, so I will tell it here.

For a long time after the voice in the night, there was little to remember about my father. There were several letters with money in them; but they were sent back. Weeks, months drifted by like fog and were sleeping years. My father became almost a leg-

endary figure for me—a part of all that vaguely used
to be and would not be again.

Also, I was growing up. My "masterpiece," *The
Divine Enchantment,* was completed at the advanced
age of seventeen. Thus, my debt for the privilege of
living a little while on this amazing planet was
finally canceled, as I fondly assumed; and now for a
triumphant reversal of the indebtedness! Why not?
Had I not been given a great dream and had not the
heavens opened for me?

Then the raucous world broke through!

The battleship *Maine* blew up in Havana harbor!
Flags waved! Drums rolled and boomed! Brass bands
blared, proclaiming the eternal glory of the Stars and
Stripes. Long trains, bulging at the windows with the
faces of singing, yelling young heroes, brawled
across the lately tranquil land. *War! War!* The grand
old race adventure was beginning again, and there
had been no such ascension of the national spirit
since Bull Run! War! There was going to be a hot
time for perfidious Spaniards. War! War! No more
humdrum living!

Then, out of the tumult and the shouting, my
father emerged, quite undramatically. There was a
postcard photograph of a stockily built man in khaki
—a member of Company L, 22d Regular Infantry,
and the regiment was bound for the Philippine In-
surrection.

"How are your Mama and sisters?" Rather a casual
message, it seemed!

For several weeks thereafter, there was no further
news.

Then a bulky letter arrived from Honolulu—a reg-
ular tourist letter, definitely literary in tone, all awe
and scenery, and laboriously embellished with or-
nate capital letters.

Nothing about the war! Incidentally, he "anticipated interesting experiences in the Philippines."

That was the last communication for months.

Then there was a bundle of Spanish newspapers tightly bound with hempen cord. Somehow it had escaped the attention of customs and arrived unopened. At the heart of the bundle was a bronze angel, six or eight inches high, with wings still spread for heavenly flight, and cheeks still plump with the trumpet-blown evangel of resurrection and love for all men!

A note tied to the angelic figure read: "From a chandelier in a cathedral of northern Luzon."

No covering letter to tell what the little angel had cost in suffering and jungle fighting.

After the Philippine Insurrection, the 22d Regulars returned to the States to be stationed at Fort Crook, Nebraska. As a matter of curious interest, I recall here that seventy years later the president of the Philippine Republic sent me a golden laurel wreath together with an official citation declaring me Prairie Poet Laureate of America.

My father received his discharge in Manila and he chose to remain there in the hope of making a new life in a new world. I received a long letter from him, setting forth the great opportunities the islands offered to enterprising Americans, especially soldiers. He had already established a livery stable for which there was a great need in Manila, and he was acquiring necessary equipment for the business.

Equipment! Horses and buggies! With a twinge of the old heartache, I recalled the astonishing cavalcade of crowbaits and rattletrap vehicles he brought home one day to the sardonic delight of the neighbors, and my secret shame.

Why not form a partnership—"Nicholas Nathan

Neihart and Son, Manila, P.I." Together we could do wonders over there, and it would be a good place for writing books. Then, when the business was well established, we could send for "your Mama and the girls." He had saved nearly all his army pay and could meet my travel expenses.

Along with the letter, he sent his official discharge, certainly a most honorable document, testifying to his excellence as a soldier. It was a prized possession, he said, and I must return it promptly by registered mail.

There was a blank space for the listing of engagements with the enemy. These were written in red ink, and there were so many of them that they spilled over into the margins, making a bloody tangle of Spanish and Filipino names, some of which had made newspaper headlines ten thousand miles away back home—Malinta, Two Angels, Caloocan, Pasig, Malolos, San Isidro, San Fernando, Novaliches, Bayombong.

I was proud of my father's record as a soldier; and the promise of adventure in strange lands was a powerful temptation. But what then seemed the greater of two contending loyalties won the struggle. Sometimes I still wonder what if I had gone.

We continued our correspondence in a desultory fashion after that; the letters becoming fewer and fewer, until we lost contact again.

And then—.

I was living in Bancroft, Nebraska, at the edge of the Omaha Indian Reservation some ninety miles north of Fort Crook where the 22d was stationed, with nothing to do but drill and remember.

A cagey lot they were—"single men in barracks" —with no social ties to mention and no relief from boredom save an occasional leave and a bit of merry hell raising in the nearby city.

During the early summer, by way of walking some of the original sin out of their systems, they had been marched to their rifle range on the Omaha Indian Reservation. I was away from home at the time, and civilians were not welcomed on the range, so I had not seen them.

It was late August when the exciting news struck our little town. The 22d was coming! The Regulars were marching back to Fort Crook, and they would camp at Bancroft over the weekend!

My father's buddies in battle! I would go to meet them, and we would march together, like old times. Surely some of them would remember Nick Neihart.

So, shouldering my little .22-caliber rifle, I set out on the reservation road leading to the rifle range fifteen miles away. It was an hour or so later when I saw the low dust cloud floating raggedly above a broken column of men plodding doggedly in rout step with Krag-Jorgensen rifles on their shoulders.

When I asked one of the first in the line where Company L might be, he crooked a perfunctory thumb to rearward and made no reply.

Twice again I received the same surly response to my question. Then, halfway down the line, I came to a sergeant who actually looked down upon me with a friendly grin. It was a good way up there to that grin, and the man was built like a battleship all the way. "Well," he said, "looking for somebody, maybe?" I said I was looking for Company L. "It's right here, Bud," he said. Then did he know a man by the name of Nick Neihart?

He leaned far down to get a better look at my face. "Did I know old Nick Neihart, did you say? Yes

I knew him—knew him all the way from Caloocan to hell-n-back! He was my buddy. Yes I knew him! And who the devil are you but his son? I'd know the cut of that jib anywhere in the world! Here, get in line! You belong to us! And let's swap guns—my Krag for that wicked-looking weepin' you're packing there. Looks dangerous, like it might go off!"

So I shouldered his Krag, he shouldered my little .22 rifle, and as veteran buddies we marched together the rest of the dusty way.

The regiment bivouacked in a pasture at the edge of our village. A chill had fallen with the late August night, and a dozen of us sat around my sergeant's fire, talking about "old Nick" for the most part. I gathered that they regarded him as quite a "character," but they liked him.

"Your dad," I was informed, "was a well-educated man (!), well posted. Could have been a sergeant or better but didn't want to be bothered. Read books, any kind he could get. Never smoked or took a drink. Said it wasn't 'wholesome'! Saved his pay too. If you needed a dollar or two, you could always borrow from Nick until the ghost walked again. Never got sick or done out on the long march north through Luzon, fighting the little brown devils. When good men were dropping out of the line, to be picked up by the bull carts, he'd be roaming about hunting mementos, by god!

"You couldn't call him a big man either. A bit short at one end; but all man at that. Like when we of Wheaton's brigade charged with bayonets across the Pazig River—or was it the Talishan? There was a mess of creeks and rivers thereabouts. We had to cross this river to take Malinta yonder on the hill. There it was in front of us, with an adobe wall (or was it stone?) all along the far bank. And back of that: the Filipinos in the trenches with their Mausers.

"That was the time we lost our Col. Harry Egbert —and a good man he was too! Things looked pretty bad, and our outfit was hanging back, with the colonel trying to get us started. When they dropped him with a slug in his belly in full sight of us there, all hell broke loose along the line. The outfit went crazy. We didn't need any more prodding. We all just took to the river, yelling like a tribe of Comanche. The water was breast deep to an average man, and there was some current, so you could hardly keep your feet. They were pouring it into us from behind that wall, and we couldn't return their fire because we had to hold our guns over our heads.

"Of course your dad couldn't wade it; but he just turned over on his right side with his rifle held up out of the water in his left hand and began swimming. I swear that man could float like a goddamn cork. Seen him out in the middle of the Pazig laying there for an hour like he was anchored!

"Most of us managed to make it across somehow, and we dug them gu-gus out of their trenches. Then we took Malinta yonder on the hill."

"Seemed he liked combat," someone remarked. "Mind the time he had himself a little war all by himself? Roaming about in the tangled woods against strict orders not to leave the column. Got to hunting queer flowers, most likely, when the Filipinos spotted him—three of them with Mausers and bolos. When the relief party arrived on the scene, they found him snugly entrenched in a swamp and ready for more trouble.

"We called it Nick's War. Heavy enemy losses, no American casualties, no prisoners.

"Got docked half month's pay for that and sent to the kitchen for a spell, besides!"

After a lapse of silence, one of the lounging men began to chuckle, breaking into lusty guffaws now and then. "Yes," he said at length, catching his breath and addressing me, "your pa was sure a curious cuss, always poking about expecting to see something new. Now this I'm telling happened a way up north in Luzon at one of them little towns with funny names, like Novaliches, maybe; but that's not it. Could be San Something, San Nicolas, San—.

"Most of the outfit was dog sick and weak as cats from what we had. Men were always dropping out of the column to make for the brush in a big hurry; and the rear guard was kept busy picking up the stragglers and herding them back into line, or into the bull carts.

"Now the way I heard, your pa was poking about, as usual, to see what he could see; and there is this nice little church all alone at the edge of the jungle. So he follows his nose inside, and there is nothing there but the altar. No, there is a jar set in front of the altar, and it is full of rice!

"Your pa thinks maybe it is a way the gu-gus have of hiding something precious from the Americanos. So he shoves his arm down into the rice, and there is nothing but paper down there. Paper is scarce in the jungle, and so your pa stuffs a bunch of it into his knapsack. Then he follows his nose about for a while longer, and there is nothing in there but the altar. So he takes out after the column.

"After awhile, the way I heard it, your pa has a call of nature, as they say, and he steps aside from the trail a decent bit, for your pa was kind of nice in his ways; and there I guess he sits awhile, thinking about when he was a carefree boy down on the old homestead. But whatever he is thinking, after awhile he thinks of the paper!

"Then, bye and bye, as I heard it, the rear guard comes along, combing the tall grass and brush for stragglers, and there they find him squatted, thinking about the old homestead.

"And the sergeant says, seeing what he saw, 'My god, Nick, do you know what you have gone and done? That's real money, soldier, and you've done used up nigh onto five hundred dollars!' "

So we went on, shooting the breeze until most of us were sprawled in sleep about a dying fire.

And the next day was the Sabbath!

God forbid that I should enjoy what, as a faithful historian, I am now required to relate. For I am a pious man and no one could deplore more than do I the sinful deeds of unregenerate men.*

Then why tell it?

Simply as a scholarly contribution to profane history, and so far as I know, it is unique in military annals.

That fateful morning the sun arose heat pale in a cloudless sky; and there was no wind. A spirit of blissful peace brooded over our innocent little village huddled among its green hills. Church bells chimed, summoning the righteous to worship. Now and then a meadowlark sang out. Drowsy cattle (I had nearly written *kine,* so bucolic was the scene)—drowsy cattle browsed lazily in the lush pastures.

Apparently all went well in the best of possible worlds.

*(!)

But it was getting hotter and hotter; and there was a battalion of brawny fighting men in yonder shadeless camp. These men had actually been drinking inordinate drafts of ordinary tepid water from a barrel—can you imagine it? And it was getting hotter and hotter. By noon, according to the most reliable information obtainable, these men were (metaphorically) spitting cotton. By midafternoon, in a manner of speaking, we are informed, they were stepping on and stumbling over their tongues.

In short, the situation had become a proverbial powder keg wanting the match.

Someone—it will never be known just who—may have spoken an idle word to his panting neighbor, quite without sinsiter intent, we assume, as to *how about a great big tin pail all covered with cold sweat and foaming full of keg beer?* Eh?

Well, what do you think? And what did the neighbor's neighbor think about it?—and the neighbor's neighbor's neighbor? What did each in turn think about it as the cruelly provocative suggestion proliferated throughout the shadeless camp?

Where to get it? That's what they thought about it! Even as a single soul they thought, so commanding was the common need. And the answer must have seemed crystal clear; for yonder dozed our helpless little village. Admittedly the contemplated act on a Sunday would break the law, both human and divine; but here was a veritable biblical ox to be pulled out of the ditch!—and it was getting hotter and hotter. So what were we waiting for? Beer! Beer! *Let's go! Let's go!*

That, so to speak, was the match!

Tin cups were passed out from the mess wagons, and the advance was on! It was not unlike the bayo-

net charge at Malinta when the colonel fell with a
Mauser slug in his belly—a ragged, headlong,
swarming surge of men driven by a single purpose.

"Beer, beer," they chanted in unison, as they got
underway and entered the main street of our town.
No officer in sight—not even a shavetail.

Daring little boys pranced proudly along the
flanks of the martial host, in their pride, half traitors
to their own. Fearful little children at furtively
opened doors peeked at the soldier men from behind
mother's hobbled knees. Windows slammed shut
and blinds came down on startled faces. Dogs barked
savagely, more in gleeful welcome than in wrath.

There must have been considerable collusion be-
tween the invaders and the natives, for all the back
doors of the saloons mysteriously opened, and bar-
rels of iced beer came rolling out, to be set up,
tapped, and spigoted in the middle of main street!

There were those who argued that this big tea
party of the 22d Regulars was, as a matter of fact,
"on the town"; and that the hostile invasion was
only window dressing for those of tender conscience.
But I don't believe it; for the assault was driven home
with such fury and determination as no amateur
playacting could simulate.

Nothing, it seemed, could stop this surging swarm
of men. The Spaniards had not stopped their charge
up San Juan hill in Cuba. Hunger, exhaustion, chills,
and fever had not stopped them in north Luzon
when the bull carts bogged down in mire and the
carabao dropped dead in harness.

Nothing, it seemed, could stop them. Even the
august ladies of the Aid Society were quite helpless.
Calling upon the town marshall, they invoked the
majesty of the law. "For heaven's sake, can't you *do*

something? This is perfectly disgraceful, and on the Sabbath too! Can't you please do something?"

Whereupon it is reported the man of law replied: "Lady, them's fightin' men and how in hell am I to arrest a battalion; and where in hell do I put them if I do?"

So the tea party went on and on, with a merry clinking of toasting tin cups and songs that were not learned at mother's knee!

The storming of Bancroft!

Truly it was a famous victory! When the medical corps arrived to glean the fallen on the stricken field, most of the casualties were reported as more or less ambulatory.

It has been noted that my father was not present at the storming of Bancroft, being, at the time, still in Manila, I believe. It was just as well so, for he would hardly have regarded the engagement as either heroic or "wholesome."

As for myself, I declare on my word that I was only an innocent and decently outraged bystander; just as I am here only the conscientious historian.

I had felt very close to my father again during the hot and dusty march with his buddies of Company L and my camping with them in the pasture that night. So when the battalion broke camp and began the three- or four-day march (90 miles) back to Fort Crook, I went a farewell piece along with them, walking beside my sergeant friend. We traded guns as before; my little .22 looking like a toy up there on his beefy shoulder, and I packing his Krag. We didn't say much. There didn't seem to be much of anything to say, not even about the big tea party. Several miles down the valley, we traded guns again, shook hands —and that was it.

Feeling lonely and forsaken, I stood there for a long while, watching the low dust cloud drift away and vanish.

The rest of my father's story is brief in the telling, insofar as I know it, although long in the living.

There was an irregular exchange of more or less perfunctory letters with frequently changing addresses, over a period of a dozen years or more. Now and then he would enclose a small sum of money in currency. "Tell your Mama to get herself a pretty new frock." (He did say *frock*.) Sometimes it was "your pretty sisters" he remembered.

Then my letter was returned by the post office. No such person known. No forwarding address given.

Most likely he was off on some hopeful and ultimately highly profitable adventure, although he must have been aging considerably by then.

There was one more letter. It bore a blurred foreign postmark and carried "warm regards for you, your Mama, and sisters."

After that, there was silence. We slowly came to regard him as dead, and he was never mentioned in our house.

I was married. There were children for whom there was no Grandpa Neihardt—only Grandma.

Then he was seen once more.

Or was he?

I was running a daily column in the *St. Louis Post-Dispatch* and the family was living in St. Louis; but my two younger daughters, Hilda (12) and Alice (8), were spending the summer with their Grandmother in Branson, Missouri.

One morning in the gray of early dawn, Hilda awakened from a deep sleep and saw, through a window opening on the backyard, a stockily built man in khaki uniform. The man was standing beneath the clothesline at a desk such as one sees in public places, busily intent upon what he was writing.

Vaguely alarmed by the sight of a strange man in the yard, she turned away and pinched herself to make sure she wasn't dreaming. When she turned back to the window, the man was still there, writing, writing, eagerly writing. Then he slowly faded into the gray of early morning; and there was only the backyard and the clothesline and the twilight.

Hilda was so mystified by her strange experience that she hesitated to tell her Grandmother. A strange man writing at a desk under the clothesline! How silly!

But Hilda, Alice, and I were great pals, having shared many adventures, and we were still able to believe many wonderful things that those who were too thoroughly grown-up could no longer believe.

So when I came down from the city on the weekend, she told me in confidence about her strange man writing under the clothesline. And as I heard, I was overwhelmed by the conviction that it was my father she had seen; that he wanted me to write and learn something of great importance to him, and he had been unable to reach me direct.

I *did* write to the War Department and learned that Nicholas Nathan Neihart had recently died in a California soldiers' home and was buried in a military cemetery near Los Angeles.

Further inquiry resulted in obtaining a widow's pension for my mother.

If Hilda's "strange man" was my father, as I believe, then apparently he was satisfied with what I had done, for he was never seen again.

15.

Homecoming of the Bride

The train from New York was now arriving on track 13. So the megaphonic voice of doom was telling the world in general (and me in particular), resounding through the great arched hollow of the old Union Station in Omaha, Nebraska. "Train number 112 from New York now arriving on track 13."

Soon I would see her for the first time with my eyes! And soon she would see me for the first time with *her* eyes!

What would I think of her—and more terrifying still—what would she think of me? I remember feeling furtively in my breast pocket for the marriage license—which I knew, almost too well, was there—indeed it was still there and had been for the past twenty-four hours.

"Train number 112 now arriving on track 13."

(My god! I thought. What have I done?)

After fifty glorifying years with her, I am not ashamed to admit I was scared. I was scared much as when, as a little boy, I spent a night away from home for the first time and wakened in the night. I wanted to get up and run!

My mother, I knew, had come down from Bancroft, seventy-three miles, the day before to be present at my wedding at the home of my friend, Keene Abbott. Keene was a feature writer for *The Omaha World Herald.* The Reverend T. J. Mackay of the Presbyterian church would be waiting for the word "go" to tie the knot that would bind us together for "ever and ever"—which seemed a long, long time at the moment. Keene, doubtlessly noting signs of trepidation in me, tried to be jocular. "Keep your tail up, old horse," he said. "It's all been done before. Even I did it with some success, you will admit!"

I had to go through with it! The man was now throwing back the big iron gates. People were crowding up, eager to meet their friends and loved ones.

"It's all yours now," Keene said. "You brought this on yourself. You must go alone and fetch her. I will be waiting here to back you up, and may God be with you!"

It was my moment of truth and I plunged to meet it. A swift memory of her first glowing letter to me thrilled and strengthened me. It came from Paris. She had read my *Bundle of Myrrh*, a sequence of love poems, which was making a stir in New York and among young Americans abroad.

The brakeman was placing the footstep on the depot platform. I remember my impatience with the first passenger to appear from the Pullman car, a corpulent lady who fussily blocked the doorway to the coach with a collection of bandboxes. The second was certainly not my Mona if her photographs were accurate. But the third! *My god, the third!*

A stately young woman of more than average height stepped gracefully through the coach door. She wore a velvet cape and her hat of like material was almost ample enough to serve as an umbrella, I thought. I recall that I felt a momentary twinge of embarrassment.

She, placing her hand upon the gallantly offered

arm of the brakeman, anxiously scanned the crowd
a moment. Then, with a joyous shout of recognition,
she shouldered her way to me, crying "John! John!"

Next day we were married. Keene served as best
man, and my mother as matron of honor. The fol-
lowing article, written by Keene, appeared in the
Monday morning *Omaha World Herald* and reached
Bancroft in the forenoon of the next day.

MARRIAGE OF AN
AUTHOR AND ARTIST

John G. Neihardt of Bancroft and
Miss Mona Martinsen of New
York Married.

Ceremony Performed in Omaha Sun-
day Afternoon by Rev.
T. J. Mackay.

Here is a partnership in art as well as a nuptial
partnership: the wedding of John G. Neihardt of
Bancroft and Miss Mona Martinsen of New York.

Miss Martinsen is the daughter of Ada and Ru-
dolph Vincent Martinsen. Mr. Martinsen was a dis-
tinguished international financier and was for some
years president of the Maxwell Land Grant as well as
of the Missouri, Kansas and Texas Railroad.

This is the initial visit of the bride to the West.
Although she is young in her art she has already had
wide recognition. It was of her, some two or three
years ago, that F. Edwin Elwell, curator of the Metro-
politan Museum of Art, said in an article published
in Arena Magazine that he considered her the most
gifted of the younger generation of women sculptors.

Words of such warm praise are, of course, to be
considered as an honor, but not to the same degree

as is the bare fact that for five years she studied under Rodin, the pre-eminent master of France whose statue of Balzac is acknowledged by art critics to be one of the most striking pieces of modern sculpture.

She is a sculptor well known in the east, but still better known abroad. In the spring of 1907 an important work of hers was exhibited in the Paris salon; it was a life-size figure called "The Maiden."

As to Mr. Neihardt, his work in the eastern magazines began to attract wide attention some three years ago. His collection of short stories called "The Lonesome Trail" received many congratulatory reviews both in America and in England, but his lyric sequence, "A Bundle of Myrrh," published a year ago is the work which has done most to bring his name into prominence.

In an essay on Mr. Neihardt's book of poems, published in Putnam's Monthly last June, Gerald Stanley Lee has the following:

"That first morning when the poems came I did not read them through. I was too happy in the middle of the book, and in the middle of the idea that there could be such a book, not to go out doors on the meadow and think about it. Think how there really was such a man, a latent, big contemporary, a possible classic, a man singing as if he were singing three thousand years ago or a thousand years on from today. After the first few pages I was too glad merely to take him as poetry. He was 'news' and there was nothing to do but go out doors with him and look at Mount Tom and the sky and the world with him, and think how it made it all over to suppose there was a man like this in it—not under a headstone visited by pilgrims and young ladies or in a classical dictionary, but walking about this minute, in the town of Bancroft, Neb."

Since then Mr. Neihardt has been placing his verse

with the leading periodicals. Last summer, for the Outing Magazine he went down the Missouri River from the head waters to Sioux City in an open boat. His descriptive articles of that journey are to be a feature of that magazine during the coming year.

A representative piece of prose fiction by Mr. Neihardt appeared over a year ago in "The Smart Set." The tale, a novelette called "The Discarded Fetish," was a character study of unusual strength which earned much favorable comment from the reviewers, both in the east and the west. He is a man of letters who, in the past three years, has been making a name for himself in the field of prose fiction and verse.

With Rev. T. J. Mackay officiating, the marriage ceremony was held Sunday afternoon at the apartment of Mr. and Mrs. Keene Abbott, 531 South Twenty-fifth Avenue. It was an informal event with no guests present aside from the mother of Mr. Neihardt.

The young couple will be at home in Bancroft after tomorrow.

The daily arrival of the evening train from Omaha was always an event in our little town of Bancroft; but this Wednesday the gathering on the station platform indicated something special was abroad. The *Omaha World Herald* article announcing our marriage and return to Bancroft must have gotten around. The assemblage on the platform of the railroad station was notably larger than usual.

As I stepped off the train ahead of Mona and offered my arm to her, I was aware that men who certainly were not given to the gallantry of hat tipping shyly touched the brim of their hats, evidently striving to make it seem quite accidental. Further it was to be observed that Mr. Cabney stood stiffly at attention against the station wall, his head bared, his hat pressed against his left shoulder. He might have been saluting the passing flag!

The city bus line, consisting of a light spring wagon, furnished with a canvas roof and cross seats, was obligingly on hand; and soon we were on our way home with our baggage. But anyone watching our progress (and who wasn't?) must have noted that the young driver was deliberately taking the longer route up Main Street where there were the most observers.

It was something of a triumphal procession. Eager faces jostled each other in the barbershop door. There was a gathering in front of the drugstore. All seats were occupied on the steps of the Cary and Ransom Farm Implement establishment. Curtains fluttered and window shades went up as we turned into the residential section of town.

And so—the bride came home.

16.

The Burning Bush

During most of my creative years I managed to arrange my life so as to realize and maintain much of the primitive relationship with earth, sky, and weather. In order to do this, we lived in a small country town and produced most of our food in the old-fashioned biblical way, by "the sweat of the brow."

All through the hot summer months we were more or less conscious of the inevitable winter and were preparing for it. This was far from being an unpleasant task. There was, in fact, a happy, prosperous, even heroic feeling about it. The deep cave in the backyard was made to preserve potatoes, cabbages, and various root crops, along with several hundred quarts of canned vegetables and fruits. I remember one autumn when I counted fourteen kinds of vegetables and fruits, raw and canned, in that cave.

Usually we had a friendly cow who was definitely one of the family, and the delightfully cold cave kept her milk and butter sweet. We had no refrigerator those days, and iceboxes were expensive luxuries. About the time of the first frost we often butchered a hog we had raised, and cured the meat.

Several years I was able to furnish all our firewood for heating and cooking.

So, before the thermometer became quite irresponsible, reporting vicious readings of thirty or forty below, we were ready for the siege of winter to begin. Let the blizzards howl! We would meet them with a roaring, red-hot stove and a cave full of provisions.

The way of life sketched here depended most of all upon a garden, and I took great pride in raising a big one that was also beautiful. It was always made considerably larger than necessary for our needs, by way of guarding against a possible poor yield; and we could always share a good crop with gardenless neighbors—which, incidentally was "good public relations," as well as a pleasure.

I was proud of my garden. We lived at the edge of town where "country" began in earnest. People used to stroll past our place on Sundays, and I liked to think they were viewing my garden, which truly was beautiful in a neat, practical way. The rows were straight; the soil was clean and in good tilth; the growing things flourished happily with the doting care they received.

My forenoons were spent in my study; and my favorite time for toiling with hoe and rake followed the one-hour nap I commonly took after lunch. Being in perfect physical condition, I enjoyed swinging the heavy hoe in the wilting heat of the afternoon under the white-hot glare of the sun. The good old biblical "sweat" made me feel like a well-oiled engine, all steamed up and champing at the throttle.

On the day I now recall, it was with such a sense of abundant energy that I was enjoying the rhythmic swing of the hoe, when something must have happened to me. I was unaware of it then, and even now I do not know what it was. As I look back, trying to remember clearly, it seems there was a still, blank place of twilight yonder—no garden, no awareness that one had ever been, no surprise, no wonderment. All that came later with memory. I was nowhere, floating in a hush of soft light.

Then—apparently apropos of nothing whatever—there was a little bush, a mere huddle of bare branches and twigs, that came swimming slowly out of vagueness into vision. It was becoming vibrantly alive with a colorless stuff like diaphanous flame lacking heat. This oozed from glowing buds along the branches that kindled, glowing with the ghost of fire. Glimmering twig ends swelled with it, stretching outward and upward with a pulse-like motion into emptiness. There it traced what I seemed to know were experimental patterns of branches, twigs, and leaves, later to be realized in the green world of living matter. These shapes flourished briefly, only to fade and fall back, shuddering, into profound vacancy.

With divine persistence the tentative pattern making went on and on—flourishing, fading, falling back to stretch forth again and again, until some of the spectral shapes held fast; and more and more survived in triumph until the little bush burned tall in ghostly splendor.

Then I was leaning on the handle of my hoe and gazing vacantly at the ground. It was like coming out of a deep sleep. There was a look of queerness in the sunlight and over everything when I gazed about me, wondering what had happened. Could I have nodded for a spacious moment out of time and dreamed such a dream between strokes of the hoe? Surely I had been hoeing happily only an eye blink since.

Now as I gazed about me in puzzlement, I became aware of a little syringa bush that lived alone on the north side of our house near the edge of the garden plot, a good fifty yards from where I stood. I knew it was there, but it was of no importance to me and was seldom noticed, being on the unfrequented side of our house. It had, so I recall vaguely, a neglected, discouraged appearance, and I cannot remember ever having seen it bloom. I am quite sure I had not seen it recently. Why then had it been singled out and so exalted in my—shall I call it a dream, since I had not slept?

I am still wondering what the experience could have meant, for always as I think of it a feeling of happy safety comes over me, and I seem about to learn something glorious to know.

Had I somehow in a flash of insight passed beyond the "outer walls of sense" and witnessed the essential miracle of growth, the creative dream at work, the divine ideal still struggling to be real and beautiful?

And last of all—forgive the daring question not irreverently asked—had I seen the "burning bush"?

17.

The Two Boys

Some years ago I was for several weeks visiting lecturer in English at a Midwestern college. In addition to giving talks on literary subjects I was expected to be available for private conferences with students on any questions that might be troubling them. That was a big order; but in the more difficult cases I could at least offer some contribution to a possible answer, pointing directions for further thinking.

One day while strolling about the campus, in search of customers I might say, I chanced to meet one of our English teachers, a sensitive, notably refined young lady with a serious problem, as I soon learned.

"I am having trouble," she confided. "My English class is studying poetry, after a fashion, and it happens that my students are largely members of the football team—a formidable fighting organization, as you know. They insist with fine scorn that poetry is effeminate, fit only for girls and sissies. I declare I don't know what to do with them, for I sometimes fear they are about to convince me too. I wonder if you can help me."

"Let me at them!" I said, "for I suspect I know what they mean; and if I do, we should be able to meet on common ground. At any rate it could be fun to try."

The class met next day. I was there when the bell rang and the last scholar slumped heavily into his seat. Having waited for the shuffling to cease, I gave forth with more boldness than I felt.

"There is a rumor floating about this campus," I said, "to the effect that some of the gentlemen in this class are inclined to look upon poetry as effeminate. Is this true, may I ask?"

The reply was a high gale of unanimous assent—*"Yes—es—es—es!"*

"Good!" I exclaimed. "I am so glad you think so, because I do too!"

Apparently that shocked them, and I waited a few moments while they searched each other's faces in surprise.

"If," I added in the hush that had fallen, "if we are thinking about the same thing; and for the moment I believe we are. But a word is not unlike a bottle that pours out what is poured in; and it might be well for us to have some sort of general understanding as to the essential content of our bottle before we pull the cork."

Here I held up my hands for inspection.

"Look at these," I said. "They are square-built, practical hands, you will observe; and if you look a little closer, you will note some old calluses upon the palms. For these have been working hands, acquainted with various tools and skills. They have helped to raise a family in their time; and they have labored hard for less than a dollar a day in the not-so-good old times when hungry men were plentiful as flies and dollars hard to come by. Through these hands I have learned something of the value and the price of things. Surely these are the hands of a practical man.

"But I have a confession to make, and I now offer it for your lenient consideration: Ever since I was twelve years old, when the direction of my life first became compellingly clear, poetry has been the glowing source and center of my interest in all things human and divine. I have even been more or less justly accused of writing it myself.

"Knowing this much about me, would you care to hear me talk a little while on what the word *poetry* essentially means to me?"

Again the reply as a gale of unanimous assent—*"Yes—es—es!"* Apparently the boys were having a good time.

"Well then," I began, "I will first tell you a little bedtime story that I made up last night while I lay awake thinking of this class."

Thereupon I told my story substantially as follows:

Once upon a time, long, long ago and faraway, there lived two shepherd boys; and they were so much alike that if either saw his image mirrored in some clear pool he thought it was the other that he saw. It even happened now and then that a whole sheep flock became confused in the matter of identities and went blatting after the wrong boy.

Their names have not come down to us, which perhaps is just as well since most likely we could not pronounce them anyway. So, as a matter of convenience, we will call them A and B.

It was not only in appearance that this likeness was so pronounced. It was in everything they saw or heard or felt or thought. For instance, A might say: "B, do you see that rabbit away off yonder on that farthest hill?" Then B would squint awhile and say: "Yes, I do see that rabbit away off yonder on that

farthest hill. It looks a little like a chipmunk. See?"
Then A would squint again and say: "Yes, it does
look like a chipmunk, doesn't it?" So thereafter it
would be a rabbit that looked a little like a chipmunk
away off yonder on the farthest hill. You see, the
boys could never disagree on any matter whatsoever.

Or could they?

Now at the time under consideration, A and B
were living in exactly the same state of conscious-
ness—the ordinary everyday commonsense state,
and it had never occurred to them that other sane
states might be possible. Nor did either suspect, as
few people do, that his effective world—the world to
which he reacted and called real—was a construction
in his consciousness from selected data of his experi-
ence. Which is to say more simply that whatever the
senses alleged was accepted uncritically and inter-
preted in keeping with the prevailing commonsense
state of awareness.

How then could they ever disagree about anything
whatever? We shall see.

It was a heavenly state of perfect mutual under-
standing that the two boys shared in those en-
chanted days of long ago. But, as Sioux warriors used
to shout to each other in the heat of battle, *Nothing
lasts but the hills!* For that matter, even hills flow as
water in the lapse of cosmic time. And now the story
must record a world-changing event in the lives of
A and B.

It was all because of little Mary Jones—a very nice
girl, although regrettably "plain" as the neighbors
would say.

On this fateful day, Mary had set out on an errand
for her mother; and she had stopped for just a mo-
ment, as she thought, at the crystal spring under the

big elm tree near the pasture gate. It was not so much
for the drink of pure cold water that she stopped, as
just to gaze into the crystal depths and to dream. The
story says she liked to do that.

Curiously enough, on the very same day, it came
to pass that B, out yonder on the hill with his flock,
became very thirsty. So he thought: I will just leave
my sheep dozing here on the hill while I get myself
a drink of pure cold water at the crystal spring under
the big elm tree by the pasture gate. So he did that;
and, the way I heard it, that is how they met.

Now, as the tale reveals, at about this time, or a
little later, B looked at Mary and—would you be-
lieve it?—she was not plain at all! She was *beautiful*,
for there was something in her eyes—in her eyes—
her eyes—.

Likewise, so we are reliably informed, Mary
looked at B, and she saw what, until then, she had
only dreamed of seeing.

Now at this breathless moment in history a mere
love story would most probably aver that, having
looked upon each other thus, they could no longer
see aught else; and there would be nothing for it but
wedding bells to ring—in the happy-ever-after era.
However, this is no light romance designed for en-
tertainment in an idle hour. It is, rather, a scientific
discourse fashioned to instruct, as shall be seen. So
now the tale returns to B, whose private world had
been shaken as if by an earthquake. There was a
sweet agony deep down in his breast, just below the
wishbone, and sometimes he could hardly breathe
because of it. He couldn't eat, he couldn't sleep, he
couldn't think of anything but little Mary and her
eyes—her eyes—.

So he thought to himself: I must go and tell A all

about this, and he will help me, I am sure, for are we not closer than brothers and are we not even ready to die for each other at any time if need be?

So B ran over across the valley to where A was watching his flock, and there he poured out his heart to his friend who was closer than a brother.

Or was he?

Alas, there was something wrong! According to the story, while B ran on and on about Mary and how very beautiful she was, A just sat there staring in open-mouthed astonishment. He could hardly believe his ears. Until that moment the two boys had always held identical opinions, especially about girls as a troublesome tribe of aborigines.

And now!

Finally, as we are reliably informed, when B was compelled to pause awhile for breath, A gazed sad eyed upon the transfigured countenance of his friend and said: "B, old man, you know I'd stick with you in any sort of fracas until my belly caved in, but surely you must be plumb out of your senses. Mary Jones is as homely as a mud fence!"

"Well, gentlemen," I said at this point, "there you have my story—a rather sorrowful one for bedtime, I allow, but perhaps its meaning may redeem it.

"And now can anyone present tell me which of my shepherd boys was right?"

After a hush of hesitation, a timid voice from the back row offered a tentative reply. "Both of them, perhaps, sir?" it questioned.

"Good!" I exclaimed. "Now we are about to arrive at a great truth. Both, indeed, were right, and both were wrong, but in very different states of consciousness. For it is not true, as we commonly assume, that there is only one valid state of awareness in which all that is knowledgeable may be known and all that can happen to us may be truly felt and adequately appraised. So long as A and B were both in the commonsense state, a sheep was a sheep, a tree was a tree, and (more to our purpose) a girl was a girl.

"But we must consider that B was undergoing an overwhelming and unprecedented experience that had changed his state of awareness and accordingly his effective world. What had been commonplace and taken for granted had somehow acquired new and exciting dimensions. What had been merely accidental and transient had developed exalting overtones of the universal and the enduring.

"Yes, B was quite 'out of his senses,' as A had observed, but for a reason unknown to A. B's experience had transcended the restricted world of the senses in which a girl was only a girl, and "plain" at that, according to the neighbors. Although he could not know it, for the first time in his life B had felt the lure of woman, the sweetheart and the mother of the race—her shielding goodness, her inherent beauty, her sacred dearness.

"But language was invented as a utilitarian device for the transfer of information; and what B was striving to convey to his befuddled pal was not at all in the nature of information to be transferred by telling. It was a profound emotional experience, somehow to be *realized and shared.*

"B's undelivered and, for him, undeliverable message was nothing less than essential poetry in our meaning of the term. The poetic art was developed through the centuries to communicate suchlike expanded states of awareness, as also were the other arts in their various guises and degrees."

Pausing here to consult my watch, I said: "As for

the devastating charge of effeminancy, we have barely time for a rapid question that, I am sure, you as advanced students can readily answer:

"If you were asked to name the two nations of the Western world that have most notably excelled in the production of great poets, which would you name?"

There were several who waved eager hands aloft.

"The Greeks?" one offered.

"The English!" declared another, as though daring a contradiction.

"Yes," I said, "the English and the Greeks indeed! And it is not written that sissies were conspicuous at Thermopylae or Marathon. As for the English, the sun never set upon the British empire in its heyday, and the Union Jack flew triumphant throughout the seven seas. The fightingest men of their times, gentlemen!"

At this point the bell rang, and the din of dismissal began. Raising my voice among the turmoil, I said, "Do you still insist that poetry is effeminate?"

The reply was a gale of unanimous denial—*"No—oo—o."*

18.

Playmates

Some wise man once remarked that the two best and most rewarding playmates are: a happy child who has not yet forgotten and a simple-hearted old-ster who has remembered again.

I have found this cryptic statement richly true, for I have shared with three generations of youngsters "the simple wisdom that is wonder." And even now as I write, oldster that I am, it is the child's heart that remembers. Much of my adult life I have played, by choice, with children; first, with mine, as soon as they could toddle and even before; and then, theirs, and now—by generous good fortune—even theirs!

I recall with belly chuckles the first time I played with one of mine. It was the year of our first baby. We slept in hammocks out under the cherry trees. I remember how the bloom came, and the green fruit, and the ripe. Then, when the woods were glorious with reds and golds, it happened.

Mona had been growing in girth for some time, and we had our unfunny little joke about a barrel going around in girl's clothing. But back of the jok-ing it was all a dear and thrilling mystery.

One evening she had gone to bed early, unusually weary with her burden. After sleeping soundly for some time, she called me to her. Taking my hand in hers, she held it close against her body.

He kicked me! I tapped upon his prison wall and,

by golly, he kicked me again! "He wants to fight," I said, "the little cuss!" I remember how we hugged each other and laughed and laughed. Silly!

And that was the first time I played with one of my youngsters. Then, when the little stranger had made it through the gates of pain, emerging into Wubdom—and what is Wubdom?

Why, Wubdom is the state of being a Wub! And what is a Wub? A Wub is a recent human arrival on this planet who is still as spineless as a bowl of apple jelly. When you hold it up with the palms of your hands on its bottom, it folds together like an accordion, slumping into a helpless puddle of baby and looking exactly as all Wubs have looked from the beginning of time, according to the best authorities.

There are various well-accredited ways of playing with a Wub. Perhaps the most popular is to tickle its belly button very gently until it removes its thumb from its mouth and remarks, "a-goo-," or words of similar import.

Another more boisterous but very effective way is to dodge in and out from behind any convenient opaque object, making expressive faces the while and shouting: "Boo-oo-oo" or its variant: "Ah-kee-cha, ah-kee-cha." This latter is generally regarded by Wubs as a perfectly killing bit of comedy, often inducing an almost croup-like paroxysm of mirth. Wubs are known to have a special appreciation for this subtle type of humor.

One should make the very most of Wubdom; for it is an evanescent phenomenon, and soon the Wub shall become tentatively erect and experimentally ambulant. Once it has completed the first nonstop inter-chair flight, it can never find the long way back to proper Wubdom again. However, so charged with memories the word may become, that it may persist as a term of endearment far across the years. I myself have known and loved a Wub with whiskers and girl Wubs with boy and girl Wubs of their own.

I think it must be their instinctive sense of the other side of things—the mystery back of the apparently ordinary—that makes children ideal playmates. They seem to know, without taking thought, that nothing in this strange riddle of a world can be commonplace.

During the years of intimate association with my children and grandchildren, I learned much that I could not disclose if I would; for it is not a matter of facts to be repeated and passed on for word-of-mouth sharing. Rather it is rich experience to be pondered and lived with.

An instance is our adventure with silence. Back of our home in Branson, Missouri, there was a deserted woodland pasture, seldom entered. Midmost within was a circular opening in a narrow valley, enclosed and made secret by a ring of tall trees. In the center of the open space a lonely oak tree stood guard. My two little girls, Hilda, nine years old, and Alice, five, had come suddenly upon the place while on one of their "play-like" voyages of exploration. Being proficient in all matters of wonder, they knew at once that this was a place of enchantment. You could tell it by the very nature of the stillness. It was more than an absence of sound. You could hear it if you listened hard, and it sent a shiver up your backbone.

They must tell me immediately about their great discovery. So they did, with much excitement. And so we went together, the three of us, to the secret place of silence. And there we huddled together and listened and heard. And the great tree listened above us with all its windless leaves.

"Unless ye become as little children!"

It was while I was playing with my son's daughters, Joan, seven, and Elaine, five, that I began to feel the rich overtones of meaning in those words.

The little girls had come for an extended visit with their Grandma and Grandpa, and we soon became inseparable companions, ranging widely in our pasture and the adjoining lonely woodland where the silence lived. Often we visited our very special friend, Roark Creek, that sang a low tune all day long. Joanie could even tell us what the song was about, for she had a natural gift in such matters.

I was working steadily on my *Song of the Messiah,* and it was my habit to pray nightly for help. "Show me the way, give me the good words—let me live until this *Song* is finished, and make it true and beautiful." It was not long until the little girls insisted on helping me pray. So the three of us, usually accompanied by my cat friend, Dr. George Sylvester Katt, were holding evening services in our pasture where an enclosure of saplings made a good sanctuary.

Soon the little girls were demanding a prayer of their own—one they could say together before they prayed separately. It must not be an ordinary grown-up people's prayer. It must be a child's prayer and it must be all Indian. So I made one. It is hardly to be described as poetry but it certainly served its purpose well.

Great Spirit, you are everywhere.
You made the lovely earth and air.
You made the creek that runs and sings,

And everything with legs or wings.
You made each blade of grass and tree,
And all the little girls like me.
So good is everything you made
That I should never be afraid.
Great Spirit, teach me what to do
So I can be as good as you.

It became a regular ritual planned by Joan and readily adopted by Elaine. After reciting the prayer in unison, with hands uplifted to the sky, they took turns praying separately, remembering all living things. With each prayer they laid a stone on a holy place, thus building an altar to the Great Spirit, as they said.

They began their prayers with the rooted ones—the grasses, the bushes, and the trees. "Give them soft ground to grow in and plenty of nice rain to drink." Next came the wings of the air: "Give them sunny skies to play in and leafy trees for rest." Then came the fins of the streams: "Give them clear, fresh water for happy swimming."

Then came the two leggeds, including men and women, boys and girls. And the four leggeds: horses, cows, goats, dogs, cats, pigs, and even mice, small though they be! "If any of these are bad, make them good; and if they are good already, please keep them so."

One evening Joan, being fresh out of animals to pray for, turned to me and said: "But Gaki, what about snakes and spiders?"

"Oh, yes," I said, "pray hard for snakes and spiders. They need all the help they can get, because nobody loves them."

Whereupon she continued: "And snakes and spiders—and lizards!"

Superficially regarded, all this might seem merely "play-like." But there were more profound depths of meaning beneath the surface. It was as though the girls were unconsciously aware of a great truth, proclaiming the unity and holiness of all life, while rehearsing their divine relationship thereto.

"Out of the mouths of babes!"

I have a cherished picture in mind that should serve to illustrate this text.

My youngsters and their neighborhood friends were fond of winter picnics, when we sat around a glowing log fire in the pasture, "making up" stories and mouthing poetry.

During the afternoon, before the occasion here remembered, I had prepared the picnic fire in a place made cozy by a shielding clump of brush and stacked wood chunks for extra fuel. By early nightfall, when the children arrived, we had a bountiful mound of glowing embers. It was biting cold a short distance from the ring of warmth, which served to increase the pleasurable sense of near comfort.

But it is the point of my story that children were not the only guests. There were four-legged "people" here and there in that pasture and under the open shed, and they were curious as to what in the world the two leggeds were doing yonder where the fire glowed. So they all came straggling out of the early dusk into the circle of cozy light, where the children sat singing.

There was Bessie, the Jersey cow, she often kissed me when I milked her of a chilly morning—an endearment not soon to be forgotten.

There was Billie, the Angora goat, with his trailing, princely raiment and luxuriant beard—clowning trickster and pest of the barnyard. Often when I was busy milking, with my face in Bessie's flank, he would steal my tobacco pouch from my hip pocket and dance away on his hindlegs, chattering with impish glee.

There was Pet, the single-footing Kentucky saddle mare, a spirited mount for a good rider, but all maternal tenderness with children.

There was Ribbon, the one-eyed pacing mare ("as easy to ride as a rocking chair"). When she squatted for full speed she could outpace an ordinary horse at full gallop.

There was Trueboy, the collie, self-appointed master of the herd, bounding and barking importantly, happy to share in the doings.

And there was my special friend, Dr. George Sylvester Katt, bouncing obliquely in and out of the adjacent brush and cutting smart-aleck capers up and down the trees.

So the four leggeds came, crashing the children's party, uninvited but heartily welcome. Nudging their way into the charmed circle of pleasant warmth, they stood with drooping heads turned inward to the glow. Urged by my youngsters to "sing poetry, Daddy, sing poetry," I did so, with all the "swells" pulled out; and the two leggeds and four leggeds listened as one. Surely, for a magical lapse of time there, we were all alike in the kingdom of heaven.

19.

Epilogue

Hilda N. Petri

There is about the last chapter of my father's "testament" *a something* that makes me think he had a presentiment that his time might be getting short. His description of the picnic around the fire with all of us children and the animals—the cow, the horses, the Angora goat, the dog, and the cat—reveals his profound belief in a meaning beneath the ordinary surface of life. It is all there: children filled with wonder; a circle with no end; the loving unity of two-legged and four-legged beings; and above it all there was poetry, a vibrant song of sensitive communion and universal communication.

With our father we learned, and later on he taught our children, to pray as Indians do, not for ourselves alone but for all living things as part of a universal scheme. When he tells about our familiar request— "sing poetry, Daddy,"—and says: "I did so, with all the 'swells' pulled out, and the two leggeds and four leggeds listened as one," he is simply stating his firm belief in the unity and holiness of all life.

Our father died 3 November 1973. Something happened shortly thereafter on Thanksgiving Day that could be taken as a posthumous confirmation of his belief in the "oneness" of things. It certainly is one of the "patterns and coincidences" about which he so often remarked: strange phenomena often, perhaps lazily disposed of as "coincidences." But was it "coincidence" or, rather, evidence of the truth in Hamlet's observation: "There are more things in heaven and earth, Horatio, than are dreamt of in our philosophy?"

In order to understand what happened on that Thanksgiving Day, we must go back more than forty years to the first meeting Neihardt had with the great Sioux Holy Man, Black Elk. It was in the summer of 1930, and the two men had been visiting for a while under the sunshade near Black Elk's home on the Pine Ridge Reservation near Manderson, South Dakota. Black Elk spoke in Oglala to a member of his family, who then disappeared into the log cabin, soon returning with a neck ornament made of buckskin. Black Elk took it and held it up for my father and my brother, Sigurd, to see. Through the Sioux interpreter, Flying Hawk, he explained the significance of the Daybreak Star sacred ornament—the star representing understanding, the bit of buffalo hide for mother earth, and, yes, the eagle feather. A large eagle feather hung from the center of the painted Daybreak Star, and indicating it, the Sioux Holy Man explained: "This eagle feather means that our thoughts should rise high as the eagle does."

Some fifteen years later the concept of the eagle once more imposed itself upon us when my father took me again as his companion and stenographer to the Pine Ridge Reservation to get the life story of Eagle Elk, a fine old Oglala Sioux. Being what my father called an "unreconstructed longhair," Eagle Elk still refused to live otherwhere than in a tent . . . the only shelter available to him that had something of the character of his real and true home, the tepee. The eagle bone whistle had been the motif for Eagle Elk's life, as one will realize from my father's "authentic tale" based upon the old man's life.* It was the source of his power, and he had been saved many times from despair when he used his eagle bone whistle or remembered the words spoken to him by an eagle: *Hold fast, there is more.*

Having lived several of his later years back in Nebraska, which claimed him almost as a native son, my father returned in October 1973 to our farm home near Columbia, Missouri, to spend what his family hoped would be his remaining years. Perhaps we did realize that our time together here was limited, for we recalled fondly many things that had happened in the past, and always sadness clung around the edges of our thoughts.

"Do you remember, Hiddy," my father asked, "the time we heard the eagle bone whistle in the middle of the night?" I did, and for the benefit of my sisters and the grandchildren gathered about, the fondly loved Grandfather recounted something of our visits some thirty years before with Eagle Elk, who called him "grandson."

My father was at that time director of information of the Bureau of Indian Affairs, and so on the Eagle Elk mission we did not camp as before but roomed in the agency building. All our talks were at Eagle Elk's tent home, however, and I recall how often we had to refill the small sheet-iron stove to ward off the South Dakota cold. It was late November, and on the day we were recalling, Eagle Elk had finished telling why he no longer had his eagle bone whistle, the source and lifelong emblem of his spiritual power.

It was our habit to retire early, so that we might rise while the Daybreak Star was still visible. This,

* *When The Tree Flowered* (Macmillan Company, 1951).

Black Elk had said, would help one become wise. Although sleep came easily that night to both of us, my father and I came suddenly awake in the early morning darkness. Bolt upright in his bed, my father called out: "Did you hear that?" "Yes," I said, and I felt an exciting chill about me in the room.

Sharp and clear and shrill—and unmistakable— we both had been awakened by the sound of an eagle bone whistle!

With his family and dearest friends gathered around him, this man, sophisticated in many areas of learning but simple in his belief in the essential goodness and beauty of life, went on to what he had believed would be "the greatest adventure of all." It was 3 November 1973, and we were very sad.

For many years our family had gathered for Thanksgiving dinner together, and always "Gaki," as we all affectionately called him, had furnished a fine turkey. The tradition would continue this year, even though he was no longer with us. And so it was. Children, grandchildren, and great-grandchildren came for Thanksgiving dinner at my hilltop home to celebrate a day made more meaningful because it would be dedicated to Gaki.

Our recent loss was heavy upon us, but somehow we felt a sense of spiritual uplift. For we, too, were aware of what Neihardt termed *the otherness of things.*

Thanksgiving Day was bright and clear. The outer world, it seemed, did not share our sorrow, did not feel our loss. A number of family members had arrived, and among them my son, Robin, when it appeared. As a boy, Robin had been an avid bird-watcher. Perhaps this explains why he saw it first of all.

"It's an eagle!" Robin called out, "A bald eagle!" We all looked up, and there it was! It flew over the house, its wings flapping in the eagle's characteristic, deep fashion. Flying counterclockwise, the eagle dipped within twenty feet of the roof, then flew off to the South, and then wheeled in his flight, again counterclockwise, and circled low over the house. Then it mounted into the sky and disappeared from sight.

My sister Alice and her daughter Lynn drove up just as the eagle vanished into the South. Excitedly we told them what we had seen.

"Why," Lynn said, "I've never seen an eagle in my whole life. . . ."

Let your thoughts rise high as the eagle does.

The "great adventure" had begun.

Other Published Works

The Divine Enchantment
A Bundle of Myrrh
The Lonesome Trail
Man Song
The River and I
The Dawn Builder
The Stranger at the Gate
The Death of Agrippina
Life's Lure
The Song of Hugh Glass
The Quest
The Song of Three Friends
The Splendid Wayfaring
Two Mothers
Laureate Address
The Song of the Indian Wars
Poetic Values
Collected Poems
Indian Tales and Others
Black Elk Speaks
The Song of the Messiah
The Song of Jed Smith
A Cycle of the West
When the Tree Flowered
Black Elk Speaks
The Twilight of the Sioux
Lyric and Dramatic Poems
All Is But a Beginning